# Palgrave Studies in Economic History

**Series Editor**
Kent Deng, London School of Economics, London, UK

Palgrave Studies in Economic History is designed to illuminate and enrich our understanding of economies and economic phenomena of the past. The series covers a vast range of topics including financial history, labour history, development economics, commercialisation, urbanisation, industrialisation, modernisation, globalisation, and changes in world economic orders.

Jane Du

# China's Labour Market, 1950–2050

The Role of Family Planning in Demographic
and Income Transitions

Jane Du
The China Institute
SOAS, University of London
London, UK

ISSN 2662-6497          ISSN 2662-6500   (electronic)
Palgrave Studies in Economic History
ISBN 978-3-031-53137-8      ISBN 978-3-031-53138-5   (eBook)
https://doi.org/10.1007/978-3-031-53138-5

Cover illustration: © Harvey Loake

This Palgrave Macmillan imprint is published by the registered company Springer Nature Switzerland AG
The registered company address is: Gewerbestrasse 11, 6330 Cham, Switzerland

Paper in this product is recyclable.

# CONTENTS

# ABOUT THE AUTHOR

**Jane Du** is Research Associate in the China Institute, School of Oriental and African Studies, University of London. An agricultural economist, Du has specialized on the political economy of Chinese agriculture, and the industry-agriculture sectoral relations and their evolution. Her publications on Chinese agriculture have ranged from Mao's collectivization to Deng's agricultural reform, and the role of agriculture in China's return to the market. Another focus of her research has been on the economic history of China's agricultural growth in conjunction with the industrial era.

# LIST OF FIGURES

# LIST OF TABLES

# CHAPTER 1

# Introduction

**Abstract** This chapter offers a comprehensive overview of the manner in which China's historical demographic trends will influence its future labour market. Additionally, this chapter undertakes a concise exploration of the challenges confronting the Chinese government in addressing population and growth-related concerns.

**Keyword** Historical population · Chinese population · Qing dynasty · Republican China · People's Republic of China · Demographic transition · Labour market

## The Decreasing Proportion of Chinese in World's Population

Over the past two centuries, the Chinese population has undergone a remarkable growth, surging more than threefold. In 1850, official source[1] recorded China's population at 414 million,[2] and a century later, in 1950,

---

[1] *The Chronicles of Qing*. 1986. Beijing: Zhonghua Book Company.

[2] Critiques have arisen regarding the accuracy of China's early modern population statistics, with concerns raised about the figures not accurately reflecting the true size of Chinese population. One of the most notable critiques comes from He Ping-ti in

© The Author(s), under exclusive license to Springer Nature Switzerland AG 2024
J. Du, *China's Labour Market, 1950–2050*, Palgrave Studies in Economic History, https://doi.org/10.1007/978-3-031-53138-5_1

it saw a gradual increase to 552 million. Today, this figure has soared to over 1.4 billion.[3] This substantial population growth can be primarily attributed to improving living standard and the gradual process of industrialization that began in the late nineteenth century. These developments provided post-World War II[4] (*hereafter* WWII and post-war) China with a robust demographic dividend. While China's population has experienced this significant expansion, it is important to note that the world's population has also grown exponentially (refer to Fig. 1.1).

During the mid-nineteenth century, the global population stood at approximately 1.2 billion.[5] Subsequently, it doubled to reach 2.5 billion by 1950 and has since surged to a record high of 8.0 billion in the present day.[6] Consequently, the relative proportion of Chinese in the world's population has gradually diminished in significance, transitioning from

1959. Additionally, Zhao Quan-Cheng's work in 1941 (both 1941a, 1941b) demonstrated that even if the official data were not statistically biased, there would still be an underestimation in the calculations of up to 10%. Zhao's (1941b) estimation for the mid-nineteenth-century Chinese population was about 430 million. For further details on this topic, please refer to Ho, Ping-ti. 1959. *Studies on the Population of China, 1368–1953.* Cambridge, Mass.: Harvard University Press; Zhao Quan-Cheng. 1941a. "Xianfeng Dong Hua Lu Renkou Kaozheng (Examination of Xianfeng Donghualu Population)." *Qilu Xuebao (Journal of Qilu)* 1: 175–190; Zhao Quan-Cheng. 1941b. "Tongzhi Dong Hua Lu Renkou Kaozheng (Examination of Tongzhi Donghualu Population)." *Qilu Xuebao (Journal of Qilu)* 2: 103–130.

[3] Unless otherwise specified, the data presented in this work have been mostly sourced from the National Bureau of Statistics of China. National Bureau of Statistics of China. (n.d.). *Zhongguo Tongji Nianjian (China Statistical Yearbook).* Beijing: China Statistics Press.

[4] World War II, spanning from 1939 to 1945, was a global military conflict that engaged the majority of the world's nations. These nations were divided into two opposing alliances: the Allies and the Axis.

[5] The data cited in this context are attributed to Lee, James, Cameron Dougall Campbell, and Feng Wang. 1993. "The Last Emperors: An Introduction to the Demography of the Qing (1644–1911) Imperial Lineage." In Reher, David S., and Roger Schofield (eds.). *Old and New Methods in Historical Demography.* Oxford: Oxford University Press.

[6] As of the end of 2022, the world population reached 8.0 billion, according to the World Development Indicators from the World Bank. For more detailed data, please refer to the specific source provided below: The World Bank. (n.d.). World Development Indicators. Washington: The World Bank. Available at https://datacatalog.worldbank.org/dataset/world-development-indicators, accessed 15 August 2023.

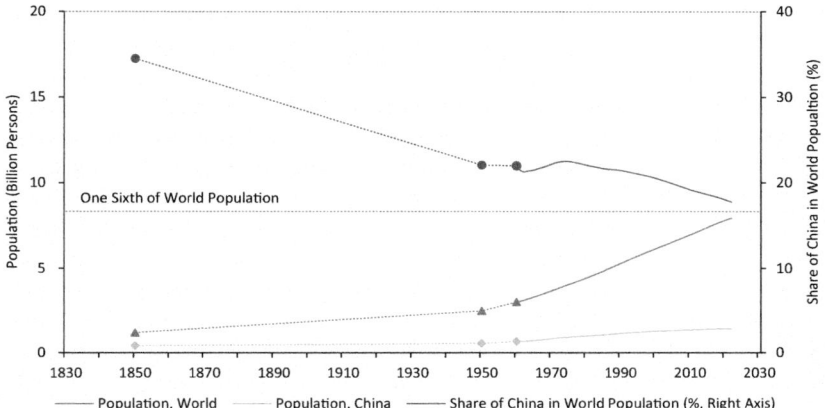

**Fig. 1.1** Historical world and Chinese population since the mid-19th century (*Source The Chronicles of Qing*. 1986. Beijing: Zhonghua Book Company; Lee, James Z., and Feng Wang. 1999. *One Quarter of Humanity: Malthusian Mythology and Chinese Realities, 1700–2000*. Cambridge, MA and London.: Harvard University Press; National Bureau of Statistics of China. (n.d.). *Zhongguo Tongji Nianjian* (China Statistical Yearbook). Beijing: China Statistics Press; The World Bank. (n.d.). World Development Indicators. Washington: The World Bank. Available at https://datacatalog.worldbank.org/dataset/world-development-indicators, accessed 15 August 2023)

being referred to as "one quarter of humanity"[7] to representing just one sixth (as depicted in Fig. 1.1).

Since the 1950s, this declining trend has plateaued due to a significant reduction in fertility rates. It is expected that China's labour market will undergo a period of downsizing in the 2020s before eventually stabilizing by the year 2050.[8] A primary driver behind this transformation is China's post-war family planning and population control policies.

---

[7] In the mid-nineteenth century, the share of the Chinese population reached as high as one third of the world's population. This information can be found in the work of Lee, James Z., and Feng Wang. 1999. *One Quarter of Humanity: Malthusian Mythology and Chinese Realities, 1700–2000*. Cambridge, MA and London: Harvard University Press.

[8] According to a population projection by the United Nations, China's population structural changes are expected to decelerate towards the late 2040s, coinciding with the entry of the first one-child generation into retirement age in their 60s. For more detailed data on this topic, please refer to Organisation for Economic Co-operation and Development

## POPULATION CONTROL POLICIES
## IN THE PEOPLE'S REPUBLIC OF CHINA

The deliberate control of the population in the PRC[9] began in the 1950s as a response to the rapid population expansion, largely promoted by Mao Zedong, who asserted that "of all things, people are the most precious in the world".[10] The substantial population size was believed to contribute to economic stagnation, especially during periods of economic downturn. Prior to the economic opening initiated in the 1980s, China experienced three significant phases of negative economic growth, including the Great Leap Famine (*sannian da jihuang*),[11] and early and late stages of the Cultural Revolution (*wenhua da geming*).[12] These challenges compelled the government to progressively implement stricter population control measures, as summarized in Table 1.1.

- The first phase of stringent population control measures was implemented during the early 1960s, coinciding with a significant decline in per capita gross domestic product (GDP), which fell by approximately 20.5% between 1960 and 1962. In response to these

(OECD). (n.d.). Historical population data and projections (1950–2050). Available at https://stats.oecd.org/index.aspx?DataSetCode=POP_PROJ, accessed 15 August 2023.

[9] The PRC was established in 1949. As of 2023, China's total population has surpassed 1.4 billion, making it the second most populous country globally.

[10] The thought, "Shijian yiqie shiwu Zhong, ren shi di yi ge ke baogui de (of all things, people are the most precious in the world), can be traced back to Mao Zedon's work, "The Bankruptcy of Idealist Historiography (*lishi weixin guan de pochan*)", which was originally published on 16 September 1949. For further elaboration on this topic, one can refer to Mao, Zedong. 1951 [1991]. "Weixin lishi guang de pochan (The Bankruptcy of Idealist Historiography)." In Mao, Zedong. *Mao Zedong xuanji* (*Selected Works of Mao Tse-Tung*) 4:1511–1512. Beijing: People's Publishing House (Renmin chuban she).

[11] The Great Leap Famine occurred in China from 1959 to 1961 and is commonly acknowledged as one of the most significant non-natural disasters in human history. The estimation of the death toll resulting from starvation during this period has been a subject of controversy. In Yang Jisheng's work "*Tombstone*", the figure is reported to be approximately 36 million. For more detailed information, please refer to Yang, Jisheng. 2012. Tombstone: The Untold Story of Mao's Great Famine. London Allen Lane.

[12] The Cultural Revolution movement in China was initiated by Mao Zedong and lasted from 1966 to 1976. The primary objective of the Cultural Revolution was to safeguard the Chinese Communist ideology by eliminating traditional elements and remnants of capitalism.

**Table 1.1** Major population control policies in pre-reform China

| Year (1) | Change in per capita GDP (2) | Keywords (3) | Formal endorsement in central documents (4) |
|---|---|---|---|
| 1960–1962 | −20.5% | Instructions on birth control | The Chinese Communist Party Document No. 698. "Instruction on Earnestly Advocating Family Planning", 18 December 1962 |
| 1966–1968 | −12.6% | To enhance the family planning work | The State Council Document No. 51. "The Report of Making a Good Job of Family Planning", 8 July 1971 |
| 1975–1976 | −3.4% | Family planning and one-child policy | *PRC Constitution* (1978), Article 53. "The state advocates and promotes family planning" and the *PRC Marriage Law* (1981), Articles 2 and 12, "One-Child Policy" |

*Note* Changes in Per capita GDP are calculated from data of National Bureau of Statistics
*Source* Du, Jane. 2017. "China's Population Policy and the Future of Its Labour Market". In Tong, Sarah Y., and Jing Wan. (eds.). *China's Economy in Transformation under the New Normal.* Singapore: World Scientific, pp. 187–200; National Bureau of Statistics. 2010. *Xin Zhongguo 60 Nian Tongji Ziliao Huibian* (*China Compendium of Statistics 1949–2008*) Beijing: China Statistics Press

economic challenges, the Chinese central government issued Document No. 698 in 1962, which aimed to promote nationwide family planning initiatives.[13]

---

[13] For details, please refer to Chinese Communist Party (CCP) Central Committee, Document No. 698. 1962. "Instruction on Earnestly Advocating Family Planning (Zhonggong zhongyang guowuyuan guanyu renzhen tichang jihua shengyu de zhishi)." Beijing: Chinese Communist Party Central Committee, 18 December 1962.

- Following the second phase of economic decline, which saw an average GDP decrease of –12.6% between 1966 and 1968, efforts to promote family planning were further strengthened. This commitment was formalized with the issuance of State Council Document No. 51 in 1971.[14] Throughout the period spanning from the early 1960s to the late 1970s, the Chinese government conducted a series of consecutive trials aimed at introducing birth control measures and advocating for nationwide family planning.

As the Chinese economy reached its lowest point towards the end of the 1970s, a large population was identified as one of the primary factors contributing to the country's prolonged economic underdevelopment. Consequently, in the early stages of economic reform, a series of new restrictive birth control policies were introduced. "Family planning" was officially incorporated into *the 1978 Constitution of the PRC*, with a firm endorsement of the "one-child policy" included in the *1981 Marriage Law*.[15]

For nearly five decades, China's population policymaking was guided by classical foundational principles, predicated on the core assumption that Malthusian growth,[16] driven by natural resource constraints, would predominantly shape China's growth trajectory. This assumption held true for a considerable period following 1949, as the Chinese economy heavily relied on the agricultural sector, and a substantial portion of capital accumulation and industrial inputs were dependent on agriculture.

---

[14] See the State Council Document No. 51. 1971. "Circular of the State Council on Forwarding on the Military Control Commission of the Ministry of Health, Ministry of Commerce and Ministry of Chemical Industry's 'Report on Better Implementing Family Planning Policy'" (Guowuyuan zhuanfa weishengbu junguanhui shangyebu ranliao huaxue gongyebu guanyu zuohao jihua shengyu gongzuo de baogao)". Beijing: The State Council of People Republic of China, 8 July 1971.

[15] National People's Congress of People Republic of China. 1978. Constitution of the People's Republic of China (1978). Beijing: The First Session of the Fifth National People's Congress and Promulgated for Implementation by the Proclamation of the National People's Congress, 5 April 1978; National People's Congress. 1980. *Marriage Law of The People's Republic of China (1981)*. Beijing: The Third Session of the Fifth National People's Congress and Promulgated for Implementation by the Proclamation of the National People's Congress, 10 September 1980.

[16] The Malthusian perspective on the relationship between population and growth exerted significant influence over China's population policymaking from 1949 through the early 2010s.

The shift towards industrial-sector-driven modern economic growth constituted a relatively smaller proportion of the overall Chinese growth pattern until the 1980s. Only with the onset of this new phase of growth, characterized by the adoption of labour-saving technologies and concurrent income increases, did demographic transitions commence.[17] However, these transitions have led to a rapid decline in China's fertility rate.[18]

## FERTILITY TRENDS AFTER
## THE STRINGENT ONE-CHILD POLICY

The prevailing perception is that China's rigorous family planning measures were introduced concurrently with the country's initiation of economic development, leading to its "peaceful rise" (*heping jueqi*).[19] Consequently, some argue that the one-child policy effectively managed population growth[20] and played a significant role in accelerating per capita GDP growth over the past four decades.

Also, it is contended that the one-child policy effectively alleviated population pressure and contributed significantly to China's rapid economic expansion following the reforms initiated in the 1980s. By preventing the births of at least 300 million individuals and lifting 200 to 400 million people out of poverty,[21] this policy had far-reaching socio-economic impacts. Subsequently, it has been suggested that the one-child policy led to the emergence of a privileged and well-educated generation known as the post-1980s and 1990s, marking a unique development in Chinese history. This demographic shift was particularly advantageous for economic growth in the 2000s and 2010s, as the first generation

[17] Liang, James. 2018. *The Demographics of Innovation: Why Demographics is a Key to the Innovation Race*. Chichester: John Wiley and Sons.

[18] Becker Gary. 1991. *A Treatise on the Family*. Cambridge, MA: Harvard University Press.

[19] China's "peaceful rise" encompasses a collection of subtle political policies designed to communicate to the international community that China's expanding economic, political, and military influence is not intended to pose any threats to the global order.

[20] Peng, Xizhe, and Zhigang Guo (eds.). 2000. *The Changing Population of China*. Oxford: Blackwell.

[21] This calculation is derived from the disparity between estimated and actual birth rates during the period spanning from the 1980s to the 2000s.

born under the one-child policy became the cornerstone of the nation's workforce.

Indeed, the one-child policy significantly reduced China's national dependency pressure[22] and allowed the country to redirect resources towards social development following the reforms.[23] This was particularly evident in the substantial reduction of the childbearing burden on young workers, thereby rendering China's labour supply, in the post-reform era, conducive to rapid and cost-effective industrialization.

Of note however, it is crucial to recognize that there exists a substantial time lag between the implementation of a population policy and its effects on the labour market within the real economy. From the moment an individual is born to the time they enter the labour force, a minimum of 18 years transpires. Subsequently, it takes another four to five decades for that individual to reach retirement age. In essence, an individual requires anywhere from eighteen to seventy years to become fully integrated into the economic framework.

Consequently, while the one-child policy effectively controlled China's population growth, a new challenge emerged as the one-child generation began to enter the labour market roughly 18 to 20 years later. At that point, China's labour supply faced the potential pressure of a downturn.[24] According to *World Population Prospects 2022*,[25] China's Total Fertility Rate (TFR)[26] had declined significantly, dropping from 7.5 in the early 1960s to 1.2 in the early 2020s due to fertility control measures.

---

[22] Cai, Fang, and Meiyan Wang. 2005. "Challenge Facing China's Economic Growth in its Aging but not Affluent Era." *China and World Economy* 14: 20–31.

[23] Li, Hongbin, Yi Zhu, and Junsen Zhang. 2007. "Effects of Longevity and Dependency Rates on Saving and Growth: Evidence from a panel of cross countries." *Journal of Development Economics* 84(1):138–154.

[24] Cai, Fang. 2008. *Liuyisi zhuanzhedian: zhongguo jingji fazhan xin jieduan* (*Lewis Turning Point: A Coming New Stage of Chinas Economic Development*). Beijing: *Shehui kexue wenxian chuban she* (Social Sciences Academic Press).

[25] United Nations, Department of Economic and Social Affairs, Population Division. 2022. *World Population Prospects 2022*. Available at https://population.un.org/wpp/, accessed 15 August 2023.

[26] TFR is a metric that represents the average number of children that would be born to a woman if she were to live through her entire childbearing years and give birth in accordance with the age-specific fertility rates for that specific region and time period. In the early 2020s, China's TFR has further declined to 1.28, indicating a significant reduction in the average number of children per woman during her childbearing years.

Furthermore, the working-age population began to decline around the mid-2010s,[27] which is expected to have an impact on labour supply over the subsequent three to four decades.

In addition, while the expansion of higher education contributes to the accumulation of human capital in China, it also presents a dual challenge. On the one hand, it enhances the nation's human capital resources; on the other hand, as the proportion of the working-age population with tertiary education grows, it exacerbates the issue of labour shortages in certain industries, as illustrated in Fig. 1.2. This, in turn, hinders China's progress towards achieving a complete economic transition.

China's TFR has remained below the replacement level for approximately three decades. In comparison with the replacement level of 2.1 to 2.2, this signifies a 25% reduction in population size with each successive generation and, consequently, a corresponding 25% reduction in the labour force expected within 18–20 years. The implementation of the one-child policy contributed to a decrease in the annual growth rate of the labour force from 3% in 1980 to below 1% in 2015, before it began to decline further. Projections suggest that this rate is poised to diminish even further, falling by another half to less than 0.5% by the year 2030. Consequently, it is expected that the effective labour supply will contract by 20% by 2050, translating to a one-fifth reduction in China's labour market.

A reduction of a quarter billion workers from the labour market would constitute an unprecedented labour decline in Chinese history, potentially leading to an unavoidable crisis in the Chinese economy if left unaddressed.

The working-age population is also of paramount importance in shaping both the consumption demand and the overall societal and economic structure. A larger working-age population contributes to greater domestic consumption capacity and enhances the potential for development and growth. Consequently, a 20% reduction in China's working-age population would curtail demand and result in fewer employment opportunities. As nationwide consumption diminishes in tandem with declining labour supply, this dual effect of reduction is

---

[27] According to the *World Population Prospects 2022*, the total number of working-age individuals in China defined as those between 15 and 64, reached its highest point at 998.2 million in the year 2015.

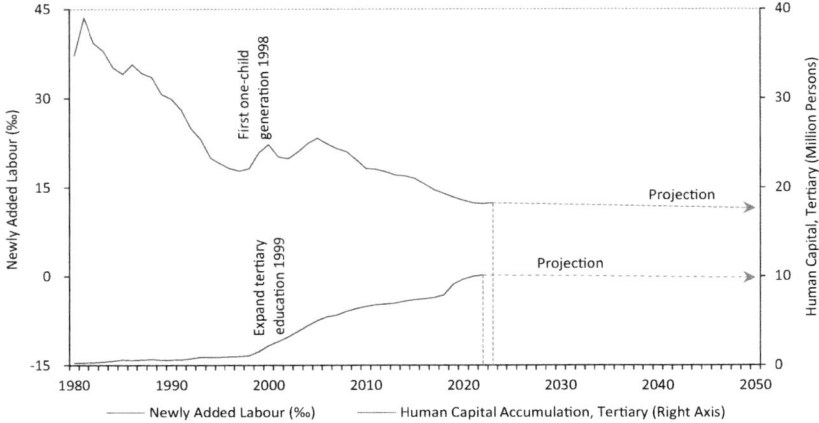

**Fig. 1.2** Labour supply and human capital accumulation in China, 1980–2050 (*Notes* The newly added labour supply was determined by calculating the population growth rate with an 18-year time lag. The projection curve aligns with the United Nations' survey data on China's forecasted population growth rate for the period spanning from 2045 to 2050. *Source* United Nations. 2001. *World Population Ageing, 1950–2050*. https://www.un.org/development/desa/pd/sites/www.un.org.development.desa.pd/files/files/documents/2021/Nov/undesa_pd_2002_wpa_1950-2050_web.pdf, accessed 15 August 2023; National Bureau of Statistics of China. (n.d.). National Data. Available at https://data.stats.gov.cn/english/easyquery.htm?cn=C01, accessed 15 August 2023)

expected to eventually trigger an economic downturn, impacting the size of the Chinese economy.

### The Two-Child Policies and the Impending Labour Shortage in China

The central government's overestimation of future fertility rates had a significant impact on China's demographic transition, especially as economic growth accelerated after 1980. When the generation born under the one-child policy entered the labour market in the 2000s, the strict population policies had a detrimental effect on the labour supply. Thus, since the early 2010s, the Chinese government has implemented measures to ease the one-child policy.

In 2013, the Chinese government initiated a relaxation of its fertility control measures, introducing the "conditional two-child policy".[28] Under this policy, couples were permitted to have two children if one of them was an only child themselves. In 2015, the government went a step further and implemented a "universal two-child policy", extending the allowance for all couples to have two children,[29] irrespective of their own birth order. Then, in 2021, the Chinese government took another significant step by permitting all married couples to have three children,[30] effectively bringing an end to the post-war population control policies.

The results, however, indicate that the two-child and three-child policies (*hereafter* referred to as the two-child policies)[31] have had limited impact on altering China's demographic trends. The birth rate has continued to decline, following a minor uptick in the period from 2014 to 2016.[32] It appears that additional factors have played a significant role in shaping fertility decisions in China. As of the end of 2022, the total

---

[28] Chinese Communist Party Central Committee, Document No. 15. 2013. "Zhonggong zhongyang guowuyuan yinfa guanyu tiaozheng wanshan shengyu zhengce de yijian (Opinions Issued by the CCP Central Committee and the State Council on 'Adjusting and Improving the Family Planning Policy')." Beijing: 30 December 2013.

[29] Chinese Communist Party Central Committee, Document No. 40. 2015. "Zhonggong zhongyang guowuyuan guanyu shishi quanmian lianghai zhengce gaige wanshan jihua shengyu fuwu guanli de jueding (Decision of the Central Committee of the CCP and the State Council on Implementing the Universal Two-Child Policy and Reforming and Improving the Management of Family Planning Services)." Beijing: Chinese Communist Party Central Committee, 31 December 2015.

[30] Chinese Communist Party Central Committee, Document No 30. 2021. "Zhonggong zhongyang guowuyuan guanyu youhua shengyu zhengce cujin renkou changqi junheng fazhan de jueding (Decision of the Central Committee of the CCP and the State Council on Optimizing Fertility Policies to Promote Long-Term Balanced Development of the Population)." Beijing: Chinese Communist Party Central Committee, 26 June 2021.

[31] From this point forward in this work, the term "two-child policies" will encompass all population policies introduced after 2013 with the aim of easing population control. This includes the conditional two-child policy of 2013, the universal two-child policy of 2015, as well as the three-child policy implemented in 2021.

[32] Following the introduction of the conditional two-child policy in 2013, China's birth rate experienced a modest yet immediate uptick in 2014, rising from 12.1‰ in 2013 to 12.4‰. Subsequently, with the implementation of the universal two-child policy in 2015, the nationwide birth rate increased from 12.1‰ in 2015 to 13.0‰ in 2016, but then sharply declined to 6.7‰ in 2022.

number of new-borns in the 2015–2022 period stands at 115.3 million.[33] This suggests that the optimistic expectations of Chinese demographers regarding the policy's effects may have been overly hopeful.[34] Nevertheless, in 18 to 20 years, these infants will enter the labour market, contributing to the growth of the Chinese economy.

In this work, data pertaining to the Chinese population size, fertility rates, birth rates, and structural ratios were sourced from various official references, including *China Population and Employment Statistics Yearbook, China Statistical Yearbook, Tabulation of Population Censuses*, World Bank's World Development Indicators and United Nations' *World Population Prospects 2022*. Policy-related materials were obtained from documents and decrees issued by the Chinese government and CCP central committee. Officially published population data and government documents are reliable sources for gaining insights into policymakers' perceptions of China's demographic landscape, or, at least, they offer valuable information to comprehend the economic reasons behind the formulation of such population policies and their associated consequences.

This work reveals that China's population policymaking has predominantly been influenced by a blend of immediate economic and political imperatives, serving as short-term objectives, as well as long-term projections derived from "academic" analyses shaped by prevailing political ideologies. However, both the long-term and short-term motivations encounter a common challenge: the sustainability of population policies over extended periods. This challenge is primarily attributable to the temporal lag between the implementation of population policies and the realization of their outcomes. A substantial portion of the effects of population policies necessitates at least one generation to manifest, during which time most of the original policymakers are no longer in positions of accountability.

Consequently, in addition to examining the total number of new-borns resulting from the two-child policies, this work highlights the significance of considering the geographical distribution of these new-borns. This is

---

[33] This figure is calculated using data collected from National Bureau of Statistics of China. (n.d.). National Data. Available at https://data.stats.gov.cn/english/easyquery. htm?cn=C01, accessed 15 August 2023.

[34] See, Shi, Renbing, Ning Chen and Qiyu Zheng. 2018. "Zhongguo shengyu zhengce tiaozheng xiaoguo pinggu (Evaluation on the Effect of Childbearing Policy Adjustments in China)." *Zhongguo renkou kexue* (*Chinese Journal of Population Science*) 4: 114–125.

essential because, in 18 to 20 years, the distribution of today's new-borns will have a direct impact on regional disparities and the composition of China's future labour market.

Recall that in the immediate aftermath of the reform, another factor that jointly shaped post-reform labour market was the intersectoral wage gap. A substantial wage differential facilitated the influx of low-wage labour into the secondary industry, facilitating the country's industrialization at a reduced cost. Therefore, while the government has to take measures to encourage childbirth to bolster the overall labour force in the future, it also needs to consider whether these newly added labour forces will be motivated to enter the industrial sector.

The current distribution of new-borns following the population easing introduced in 2013 raises the latter concern. In many labour-sending provinces in China,[35] the two-child policies have had a limited effect on altering local fertility rates. A majority of new-borns have been delivered in affluent regions characterized by a low desire for geographic mobility. In contrast, children born in less developed areas are more inclined to enter the industrial sector, primarily because per capita income in economically advanced regions often surpasses the wage rates in their home regions.

Hence, the response of the population easing measures underscores that while the two-child policies may help mitigate future labour market pressure in China, the current distribution of fertility still raises doubts about their effectiveness in addressing the impending shortage of industrial labour during China's ongoing economic transition.

---

[35] The calculation of provincial population outflows is based on data obtained from the fifth, sixth, and seventh Chinese population censuses. For more specific information, please refer to the Population Census Office of the State Council, and the Department of Population and Employment of the National Bureau of Statistics of China. 2002. *Tabulation of Population Censuses of People's Republic of China 2000*. Beijing: China Statistics Press. Population Census Office of the State Council, and the Department of Population and Employment of the National Bureau of Statistics of China. 2012. *Tabulation of Population Censuses of People's Republic of China 2010*. Beijing: China Statistics Press. Population Census Office of the State Council, and the Department of Population and Employment of the National Bureau of Statistics of China. 2022. *Tabulation of Population Censuses of People's Republic of China 2020*. Beijing: China Statistics Press.

## *Organizational Framework of the Study*

Following an examination of how China's historical demographic trends will influence its future labour market in this chapter, this work will proceed to delve into an investigation of the challenges confronted by China's central policymakers as they grapple with population and growth-related issues. To grasp the intricate interplay between contemporary China's demographics and their impact on economic matters, it becomes imperative to trace back to uncover the deep-seated historical factors and shaping forces at play.

Chapter 2 engages in a policy study aimed at tracking the progression of population policies in China. Its objective is to elucidate the pivotal factors that have influenced the formulation of these policies, particularly those influenced by the central government's stance on capital-labour ratios, as China navigated the complexities and challenges in developing a modern industrial sector. Simultaneously, by analysing the distinct feature of China's long-term population policy shifts since 1949, Chapter 2 elucidates how varying economic conditions have shaped the perspectives of core party members on the stimulation and/or regulation of birth rates and fertility. This analysis takes into account economic constraints, including the adequacy of industrial capital accumulation.

Chapter 2 also conducts an in-depth examination of the one-child policy and endeavours to identify its dual impact on China's social development and income transition. The one-child policy undeniably alleviated the burden of childbearing and dependency on young labourers from the 1980s to the 2000s. This, in turn, facilitated China's rapid industrialization by ensuring a continuous inflex of labour, propelling the nation into global economic prominence. However, following a pivotal shift in labour structure in the 2010s, the supply of labour and the working-age ratio began to deteriorate as the one-child generation reached childbearing age. This decline is expected to be as quickly as their initial rise during the early stages of reform and is expected to persist until the one-child generation enters retirement age in the 2040s and 2050s. Consequently, as the ongoing demographic changes unfold, China will increasingly grapple with challenges in manpower supply, impeding its ability to sustain economic development and achieve income transition.

Drawing from policy studies and empirical analysis tracing back to the inception of Mao's China, Chapter 2 revisits the two primary focal points of this work. It places particular emphasis on the first one: demographic transition. This chapter aims to elucidate the historical circumstances that led to the adoption of specific demographic policies, aligning them with the prevailing economic conditions and policy objectives of their respective eras.

Chapter 3 undertakes a comparative analysis of the post-war economic development and income transitions in China, as well as selected Asian economies, with a particular focus on Japan and South Korea. The objective is to examine the demographic conditions prevalent in these countries during their transition from middle-income to high-income status. It is noteworthy that, akin to China, both Japan and South Korea witnessed a decline in birth rates and fertility levels, transitioning from high birth rates to low birth rates and eventual population declines. However, a significant divergence emerges when considering the age structure of their populations during their transitions. Japan, for instance, achieved upper-middle-income status in 1968 and subsequently advanced to high-income status in 1977, all while its population structure continued to be dominated by a substantial cohort of young and middle-aged individuals in the working-age bracket. Similarly, South Korea's rapid economic development in 1988, when it reached upper-middle-income status, was largely attributed to the significant growth of its youthful and middle-aged workforce, accompanied by a low dependency ratio at the time.

Chapter 3 highlights China's current situation in its dual transitions. Compared to its neighbouring countries, China has remained in upper-middle-income group when the country's working-age ratio starts to decline. When two Asian Tigers—Japan and South Korea—faced an ageing society problem with a large proportion of population older than 65, they had already upgraded to high-income economies. But for China, this is not the case. The absence of sufficient labour supply since the late 2010s could be likely an interception process which may offset China's economic momentum. In addition, the fast expansion of higher education helped to accumulate human capital in China, but the downside is that when the share of labour with tertiary education increases, the problem of industrial worker shortage may worsen.

Considering that the ultimate objective of the two-child policies is to help China alleviate the impending labour shortage, and even though the easing policies have, to some extent, addressed labour market supply, a lingering question remains: Will these newly added labour forces, 18–20 years down the line, be effectively integrated into the industrial sector, thereby facilitating China's seamless transition to the high-income category?

The answer to this question can be partly found in Chapter 4. In Chapter 4, the empirical study on demographic and economic transitions is expanded to include an interregional comparison within China. Through this analysis of regional variations, Chapter 4 reveals that China's regional disparities in birth desire and fertility have become increasingly pronounced since the relaxation of the one-child policy in 2013. The income disparities that drive labour migration have jointly contributed to divergent responses in birth rates to the population easing policies, resulting in an overall negative change in the national birth rate, which is on a declining trend. Upon closer examination, it becomes evident that rural areas in China and regions adjacent to the prosperous coastal tier one provinces have demonstrated a positive response in birth rates to the population easing policies. Nevertheless, these interregional birth disparities among different families have not translated into a substantial increase in nationwide births. This is partly because rapid urbanization has increased the affordability of additional children for rural populations, while simultaneously shrinking the overall population base with a higher desire for fertility, driven by rising incomes in urban China.

Chapter 4 also provides valuable perspectives on how Chinese families make decisions regarding fertile behaviours. It is noteworthy that the relaxation of population policies after 2013 has had minimal impact on China's nationwide birth rate change, as discussed in this chapter. Additionally, Chapter 4 underscores that the two-child policies have been implemented uniformly across the nation, without taking into account regional variations at the central government level. For less developed regions within China, the easing of the one-child policy alone may not be sufficient to boost fertility rates. Income limits have exerted substantial influence on fertility decisions in these areas, and addressing this issue may require the Chinese government to consider measures aimed at subsidizing the costs associated with childbearing in these regions.

Chapter 5 serves as a comprehensive summary of the implications of China's population policies post-1949 on the transformation of its age structure and labour market supply. This assessment takes place within the context of the broader economic transition that began in earnest in 1979. The evolution of China's population policies has provided insights into the interplay between short-term economic factors, particularly capital input driven by industries, and the long-term consequences on demographic structure, which fundamentally alters labour supply and exerts a profound and enduring impact on growth patterns. This concluding chapter engages in a retrospective examination, consolidating the key issues discussed throughout the work, offering a comprehensive overview of the significant themes and findings explored in the preceding chapters.

Following the introduction, in Chapter 2, the focus shifts to pre-reform China's population structure and fertility trends. By scrutinizing the demographic changes that occurred in China before the reform era, Chapter 2 aims to discern the distinctive attributes of population policy formulation. It seeks to uncover the specific traits of population policy-making that have influenced the current features of the labour market in China and the challenges it presently confronts.

## References

Becker Gary. 1991. *A Treatise on the Family*. Cambridge, MA: Harvard University Press.

Cai, Fang, and Meiyan Wang. 2005. "Challenge Facing China's Economic Growth in its Aging but not Affluent Era." *China and World Economy* **14**: 20–31.

Cai, Fang. 2008. *Liuyisi zhuanzhedian: zhongguo jingji fazhan xin jieduan* (*Lewis Turning Point: A Coming New Stage of Chinas Economic Development*). Beijing: *Shehui kexue wenxian chuban she* (Social Sciences Academic Press).

Chinese Communist Party Central Committee, Document No. 698. 1962. "Instruction on Earnestly Advocating Family Planning (Zhonggong zhongyang guowuyuan guanyu renzhen tichang jihua shengyu de zhishi)." Beijing: Chinese Communist Party Central Committee, 18 December 1962.

Chinese Communist Party Central Committee, Document No. 15. 2013. "Zhonggong zhongyang guowuyuan yinfa guanyu tiaozheng wanshan shengyu zhengce de yijian (Opinions Issued by the CCP Central Committee and the State Council on 'Adjusting and Improving the Family Planning Policy')." Beijing: 30 December 2013.

Chinese Communist Party Central Committee, Document No. 40. 2015. "Zhonggong zhongyang guowuyuan guanyu shishi quanmian lianghai zhengce gaige wanshan jihua shengyu fuwu guanli de jueding (Decision of the Central Committee of the CCP and the State Council on Implementing the Universal Two-Child Policy and Reforming and Improving the Management of Family Planning Services)." Beijing: Chinese Communist Party Central Committee, 31 December 2015.

Chinese Communist Party Central Committee, Document No 30. 2021. "Zhonggong zhongyang guowuyuan guanyu youhua shengyu zhengce cujin renkou changqi junheng fazhan de jueding (Decision of the Central Committee of the CCP and the State Council on Optimizing Fertility Policies to Promote Long-Term Balanced Development of the Population)." Beijing: Chinese Communist Party Central Committee, 26 June 2021.

Du, Jane. 2017. "China's Population Policy and the Future of Its Labour Market." In Tong, Sarah Y., and Jing Wan. (eds.). *China's Economy in Transformation under the New Normal*. Singapore: World Scientific

Ho, Ping-ti. 1959. *Studies on the Population of China, 1368–1953*. Cambridge, Mass.: Harvard University Press.

Lee, James, and Feng Wang. 1999. *One Quarter of Humanity: Malthusian Mythology and Chinese Realities, 1700–2000*. Cambridge, MA and London.: Harvard University Press.

Lee, James, Cameron Dougall Campbell, and Feng Wang. 1993. "The Last Emperors: An Introduction to the Demography of the Qing (1644–1911) Imperial Lineage." In Reher, David S., and Roger Schofield (eds.). *Old and New Methods in Historical Demography* Oxford: Oxford University Press.

Li, Hongbin, Yi Zhu and Junsen Zhang. 2007. "Effects of Longevity and Dependency Rates on Saving and Growth: Evidence from a Panel of Cross Countries." *Journal of Development Economics* 84(1):138–154.

Liang, James. 2018. *The Demographics of Innovation: Why Demographics is a Key to the Innovation Race*. Chichester: John Wiley and Sons.

Mao, Zedong. 1951 [1991]. "Weixin lishi guang de pochan (The Bankruptcy of Idealist Historiography)." In Mao, Zedong. *Mao Zedong xuanji* (*Selected Works of Mao Tse-Tung*) 4:1511–1512. Beijing: People's Publishing House (Renmin chuban she).

National Bureau of Statistics. 2010. *Xin Zhongguo 60 Nian Tongji Ziliao Huibian* (*China Compendium of Statistics 1949–2008*) Beijing: China Statistics Press.

National People's Congress of People Republic of China. 1978. Constitution of the People's Republic of China (1978). Beijing: The First Session of the Fifth National People's Congress and Promulgated for Implementation by the Proclamation of the National People's Congress, 5 April 1978.

National People's Congress. 1980. *Marriage Law of The People's Republic of China (1981)*. Beijing: The Third Session of the Fifth National People's Congress and Promulgated for Implementation by the Proclamation of the National People's Congress, 10 September 1980.

National Bureau of Statistics of China. (n.d.). National Data. Available at https://data.stats.gov.cn/english/easyquery.htm?cn=C01, accessed 15 August 2023.

National Bureau of Statistics of China. (n.d.). *Zhongguo Tongji Nianjian (China Statistical Yearbook)*. Beijing: China Statistics Press.

Organisation for Economic Co-operation and Development (OECD). (n.d.). Historical population data and projections (1950–2050). Available at https://stats.oecd.org/index.aspx?DataSetCode=POP_PROJ, accessed 15 August 2023.

Peng, Xizhe, and Zhigang Guo (eds.). 2000. *The Changing Population of China*. Oxford: Blackwell.

Population Census Office of the State Council, and the Department of Population and Employment of the National Bureau of Statistics of China. 2002. *Tabulation of Population Censuses of People's Republic of China 2000*. Beijing: China Statistics Press.

Population Census Office of the State Council, and the Department of Population and Employment of the National Bureau of Statistics of China. 2012. *Tabulation of Population Censuses of People's Republic of China 2010*. Beijing: China Statistics Press.

Population Census Office of the State Council, and the Department of Population and Employment of the National Bureau of Statistics of China. 2022. *Tabulation of Population Censuses of People's Republic of China 2020*. Beijing: China Statistics Press.

Shi, Renbing, Ning Chen and Qiyu Zheng. 2018. "Zhongguo shengyu zhengce tiaozheng xiaoguo pinggu (Evaluation on the Effect of Childbearing Policy Adjustments in China)." *Zhongguo renkou kexue (Chinese Journal of Population Science)* 4: 114–125.

State Council Document No. 51. 1971. "Circular of the State Council on Forwarding on the Military Control Commission of the Ministry of Health, Ministry of Commerce and Ministry of Chemical Industry's 'Report on Better Implementing Family Planning Policy'" (Guowuyuan zhuanfa weishengbu junguanhui shangyebu ranliao huaxue gongyebu guanyu zuohao jihua shengyu gongzuo de baogao)". Beijing: The State Council of People Republic of China, 8 July 1971.

*The Chronicles of Qing*. 1986. Beijing: Zhonghua Book Company.

The World Bank. (n.d.). World Development Indicators. Washington: *The World Bank*. Available at https://datacatalog.worldbank.org/dataset/world-development-indicators, accessed 15 August 2023.

United Nations, Department of Economic and Social Affairs, Population Division. 2022. *World Population Prospects 2022*. Available at https://population.un.org/wpp/, accessed 15 August 2022.

United Nations. 2001. *World Population Ageing, 1950–2050*. https://www.un.org/development/desa/pd/sites/www.un.org.development.desa.pd/files/files/documents/2021/Nov/undesa_pd_2002_wpa_1950-2050_web.pdf, accessed 15 August 2023.

Yang, Jisheng. 2012. Tombstone: The Untold Story of Mao's Great Famine. London Allen Lane.

Zhao Quan-Cheng. 1941a. "Xianfeng Dong Hua Lu Renkou Kaozheng (Examination of Xianfeng Donghualu Population)." *Qilu Xuebao* (*Journal of Qilu*) 1: 175–190.

Zhao Quan-Cheng. 1941b. "Tongzhi Dong Hua Lu Renkou Kaozheng (Examination of Tongzhi Donghualu Population)." *Qilu Xuebao* (*Journal of Qilu*) 2: 103–130.

# CHAPTER 2

# A Concentrated Demographic Transition

**Abstract** This chapter introduces some perspectives on China's population policy decision-making process, offering an examination of the repercussions of China's post-1949 population policies on evolving age structure and labour market supply, particularly within the context of the post-1979 economic transition. Furthermore, this chapter delves into an investigation of the one-child policy, aiming to discern its dual effects, encompassing both positive and negative aspects, on China's social development and income transition.

**Keywords** Concentrated demographic transition · Family planning · Population policymaking · Total fertility rate · Dependency ratio · One-child policy · Working-age ratio · Demographic dividend

J. Du, *China's Labour Market, 1950–2050*, Palgrave Studies in Economic History, https://doi.org/10.1007/978-3-031-53138-5_2

## Comprehending China's Post-War Population Policymaking

After the end of WWII and the Chinese Civil War (*guogong neizhan*),[1] China's economic growth gradually began to recover. As living standards improved during the post-war recovery period,[2] China experienced a significant increase in its population size.[3] Mao Zedong's perspective on population, encapsulated in the phrase "with many people, strength is great" (*renduo liliang da*), succinctly set the tone for population policies during the early stages of the nation's development.[4] By the time of the inaugural national population census conducted in 1953–1954, China's total population has reached a staggering 602.7 million (as presented in Table 2.1).[5]

As the competition for employment opportunities intensified, a significant challenge emerged in the early 1950s,[6] characterized by the tension between a rapidly expanding population and the sluggish pace of job

---

[1] The Chinese Civil War was a protracted military conflict that unfolded between the CCP and the Republic of China led by the Kuomintang. This conflict spanned from 1945 to 1949 and ultimately culminated in the establishment of the RPC.

[2] Soviet technical assistance provided to the PRC played an important role in the reconstruction and development of Chinese economy beginning in 1950. For an in-depth exploration of this subject, one can refer to Heoffding, Oleg. 1963. "Sino-Soviet Economic Relations, 1959–1962." *Communist China and the Soviet Bloc* 349:94–105; and Polaris, Jean. 1964. "The Sino-Soviet Dispute: Its Impact on China." *International Affairs* 40(4):647–658.

[3] During China's post-war recovery period from 1949 to 1953, the average birth rate stood at 37.0%, and the natural population growth rate was recorded at 19.6%.

[4] Mao Zedong underscored the significance of population in the context of socialist construction, expressing the belief that "as long as there are people, every kind of miracle can be performed". Similar sentiments and elaborations on this perspective can be found in Mao, Zedong. 1951 [1991]. "Weixin lishi guang de pochan (The Bankruptcy of Idealist Historiography)." In Mao, Zedong. *Mao Zedong xuanji* (*Selected Works of Mao Tse-Tung*) 4:1511–1512. Beijing: Renmin chuban she (People's Publishing House).

[5] In 1949, the total population of China stood at 541.7 million. By 1954, China's total population had experienced an increase of 11.3% compared to the 1949 level.

[6] The years from 1953 to 1957 are commonly referred to as the era of "socialist transformation" (*shehui zhuyi gaizao*), which aligned with the implementation of the First Five-Year Plan (*di yi ge wunian jihua*). This period marked the commencement of industrialization following the establishment of the PRC. During this phase, a robust state-led apparatus demonstrated its effectiveness in directing resources towards the development of heavy industries.

**Table 2.1**   Population growth from 1949 to 1979

| Year | Birth Rate (‰) | Mortality Rate (‰) | Natural Increase Rate (‰) | Total Population (Million Persons) |
|------|------|------|------|------|
| (1) | (2) | (3) | (4) | (5) |
| 1949 | 36.0 | 20.0 | 16.0 | 541.7 |
| 1950 | 37.0 | 18.0 | 19.0 | 552.0 |
| 1951 | 37.8 | 17.8 | 20.0 | 563.0 |
| 1952 | 37.0 | 17.0 | 20.0 | 574.8 |
| 1953 | 37.0 | 14.0 | 23.0 | 588.0 |
| 1954 | 38.0 | 13.2 | 24.8 | 602.7 |
| 1955 | 32.6 | 12.3 | 20.3 | 614.7 |
| 1956 | 31.9 | 11.4 | 20.5 | 628.3 |
| 1957 | 34.0 | 10.8 | 23.2 | 646.5 |
| 1958 | 29.2 | 12.0 | 17.2 | 659.9 |
| 1959 | 24.8 | 14.6 | 10.2 | 672.1 |
| 1960 | 20.9 | 25.4 | –4.6 | 662.1 |
| 1961 | 18.1 | 14.3 | 3.8 | 658.6 |
| 1962 | 37.2 | 10.1 | 27.1 | 673.0 |
| 1963 | 43.6 | 10.1 | 33.5 | 691.7 |
| 1964 | 39.3 | 11.6 | 27.8 | 705.0 |
| 1965 | 38.0 | 9.5 | 28.5 | 725.4 |
| 1966 | 35.2 | 8.9 | 26.3 | 745.4 |
| 1967 | 34.1 | 8.5 | 25.7 | 763.7 |
| 1968 | 35.8 | 8.3 | 27.5 | 785.3 |
| 1969 | 34.3 | 8.1 | 26.2 | 806.7 |
| 1970 | 33.6 | 7.6 | 26.0 | 829.9 |
| 1971 | 30.7 | 7.3 | 23.4 | 852.3 |
| 1972 | 29.9 | 7.7 | 22.3 | 871.8 |
| 1973 | 28.1 | 7.1 | 21.0 | 892.1 |
| 1974 | 25.0 | 7.4 | 17.6 | 908.6 |
| 1975 | 23.1 | 7.4 | 15.8 | 924.2 |
| 1976 | 20.0 | 7.3 | 12.7 | 937.2 |
| 1977 | 19.0 | 6.9 | 12.1 | 949.7 |
| 1978 | 18.3 | 6.3 | 12.0 | 962.6 |
| 1979 | 17.8 | 6.2 | 11.6 | 975.4 |

*Source* National Bureau of Statistics of China. (n.d.). *Zhongguo Tongji Nianjian* (*China Statistical Yearbook*). Beijing: China Statistics Press

creation. In response to this issue, government officials such as Deng

Yingchao and Deng Xiaoping,[7] as well as social scientists (e.g. Ma Yinchu),[8] proposed the implementation of birth control and family planning measures to manage the burgeoning population.[9]

In 1955, a symbolic central document addressing the issue of birth control was released by the CCP Central Committee and Ministry of Health.[10] In subsequent years, there were additional policy declarations emphasizing the necessity of population control in the context of economic growth. Notably, the state's concerns regarding food security also encompassed population control as an integral component of its policymaking efforts.

During the initial stages of discussions within the upper echelons of the CCP regarding population issues, the concept of family planning emerged as a proposed measure. The initial implementation of

[7] In 1954, Deng Yingchao (1904–1992), who served as the vice-chairwoman of the Women's Federation, wrote a letter to Deng Xiaoping, who was then the secretary general of the CCP. In her letter, she raised concerns about "increasing demand for contraceptive devices among women cadres that was not being adequately met". Deng Xiaoping replied positively to her suggestion. For more detailed information on this historical correspondence, please refer to Scharping, Thomas. 2003. *Birth Control in China 1949–2000: Population Policy and Demographic Development.* London: Routledge.

[8] In 1957, the prominent social scientist Ma Yinchu presented the perspective that population reproduction should be seamlessly integrated into China's socialist planned system. In his work titled "Xin renkou lun (The New Population Theory)", he argued that "Chinese population grew by 2% per year in the first four years after the establishment of PRC, ... the country's population would reach 1.6 billion in 50 years (if without proper control). Population growth at such a rapid rate would definitely incur severe conflicts (with social development)". However, Ma's viewpoint faced suppression during the late 1950s political campaign, and he was subsequently labelled as a political rightist (*youpai*). For more comprehensive details on this matter, please refer to Ma, Yinchu. 1957. "Xin renkou lun (The New Population Theory)." *Renmin ribao (People's Daily)*, published on 5 July 1957.

[9] During the same period, there was an active debate concerning China's population policies. To delve into this debate further, also see Ruoshui. 1959. "Renkou yu renshou (Population and Manpower)." *Renmin ribao (People's Daily)*, 15 April 1959.

[10] The publication of CCP Central Committee Document No. 45 in 1955, dated 1 March 1955, marked the beginning of China's six-decade-long journey into birth control and population management policies. See, Chinese Communist Party Central Committee and the Ministry of Health, Document No. 45. 1955. "Zhonggong zhongyang dui weisheng bu dangzu guanyu jiezhi shengyu wenti de baogao de pishi (Instructions of the CCP Central Committee on the report of the Ministry of Health' Party Committee on the Issues of Birth Control)". Beijing: Chinese Communist Party Central Committee and the Ministry of Health, 1 March 1955.

family planning policies led to a significant decline in China's birth rate after its first peak in the mid-1950s.[11] However, the momentum surrounding population-related discussions was interrupted by the Anti-Rightist Campaign ( *fanyou yundong*) in 1957. This campaign dampened the discourse on population problems, and the family planning policy was temporarily lifted during the economic turmoil that accompanied the Great Leap Famine.[12] As a result, the net population growth rate, after the period of socialist transformation and the First Five-Year Plan, decreased from 24.8% in 1954 to 17.2% in 1958 as indicated in Table 2.1.

The population dynamics in China underwent a significant transformation during the Great Leap Famine. This period witnessed negative population growth, primarily due to two key factors: an unprecedentedly high mortality rate and a sharp decline in the fertility rate.[13] The central leadership's efforts to address this crisis included the implementation of partial de-collectivization ( *qu jiti hua*) in the food sector, a notable decision made during the 7,000 Cadres Conference ( *qi qian ren dahui*) in 1962.[14] As a result, food production and supply exhibited positive

---

[11] The crude birth rate in China experienced a notable decline, dropping from its peak of 38.0% in 1954 to 24.8% in 1959.

[12] Between 1954 and 1957, China initiated its first phase of family planning, with a particular focus on promoting contraception among women cadres. However, this effort was abruptly halted during the Anti-Rightist campaign, which was launched by the central leadership of the CCP central in 1958. Subsequently, from 1958 to 1961, during the Great Leap Forward ( *da yue jin*) period, Mao Zedong re-emphasised the advantages of maintaining a large population of 600 million for the Chinese nation. This renewed emphasis on population size took precedence over family planning initiative. The initial efforts related to family planning and discussions regarding China's population control were effectively suppressed by both political struggles and the significant social turmoil experienced during the years 1958–1962.

[13] The year 1960 marked the only instance of population decline in China since 1949. In comparison with population figures for 1959, the Chinese population experienced a notable decrease in 1960, declining by 4.6%.

[14] In the early 1960s, under the leadership of figures like Liu Shaoqi and Deng Xiaoping, there was a concerted effort to reverse Mao Zedong's rapid push towards socialism. The People's Communes ( *renmin gongshe*) underwent substantial restructuring and downsizing, and farmers were granted the opportunity to cultivate their own small plots of land and engage in local market activities. The reforms led by Liu and Deng in the early 1960s played a crucial role in ending the famine and fostering economic recovery before the onset of the Cultural Revolution.

responses in 1963,[15] effectively ending the famine and setting the stage for population recovery in the mid-1960s. Subsequent to the restoration of food production, the population began to expand rapidly.[16] The "baby boom" experienced in the early 1960s was primarily attributed to delayed compensatory births stemming from the famine period and a return to traditional, uncontrolled high-level fertility in China. By the time of the second national population census conducted in 1964–1965, the Chinese population had grown to a staggering reached 725.4 million, as detailed in Table 2.1.

The acceleration in population growth was indeed viewed as a contributing factor to the sluggish pace of economic growth in China. Coupled with the protracted economic stagnation that spanned from the Great Leap Forward through the Cultural Revolution, the debate regarding the contradiction between population size and the level of economic development remained a heated topic in China. This issue underscored the complex interplay between demographic factors and economic progress during that period.

Family planning became an integral component of China's national economic development plan with the release of Document No. 51 in 1971.[17] Although family planning policies during the early to mid-1970s

---

[15] During this period, China witnessed a significant increase in grain output. Specifically, grain production rose from 136.5 million tonnes in 1961 to 165.7 million tonnes in 1963, and it continued to climb to 194.5 million tonnes in 1965.

[16] The failure of People's Communes and the resulting food shortages greatly concerned the central government, prompting a shift back towards population control measures. In central document No. 698 issued in 1962, the Chinese government announced its "earnest" intention to implement planned reproduction. Subsequently, the central government set a target to reduce population growth to 1% or below by the end of the twentieth century, as mentioned in Liang and Lee 2012. This document marked a significant milestone as it formally endorsed family planning as a national policy for the first time in China. In 1964, the Committee on Planned Births ( *jihua shengyu weiyuanhui*) was established as an institution responsible for family planning at all levels, extending down to the local authorities. However, in 1968, amid the Cultural Revolution, the committee was dissolved. Refer to Chinese Communist Party Central Committee, Document No. 698. 1962. "Zhonggong zhongyang guowuyuan guanyu renzhen tichang jihua shengyu de zhishi (Instruction on Earnestly Advocating Family Planning)." Beijing: Chinese Communist Party Central Committee, 18 December 1962; Liang, Jianzhang and Jianxin Li. 2012. *Zhongguo ren taiduo le ma? ( Too Many People in China?).* Beijing: Social Sciences Academic Press.

[17] State Council of People Republic of China. Document No. 51. 1971. "Guowuyuan zhuanfa weishengbu junguanhui shangyebu ranliao huaxue gongyebu guanyu zuohao

were not as stringent as those implemented later, they were nevertheless compulsory.[18] As a result of these policies, there was a steep decline in fertility rates during the years 1967 to 1975. The TFR dropped from 6.3 in 1967 to 3.2 in 1977 (see Fig. 2.1), particularly in urban China.[19] However, even with this significant reduction in fertility, the Chinese population continued to grow due to the cumulative effects of several decades of previous growth. By the end of the 1970s, the Chinese population had reached approximately 975.4 million, as shown in Table 2.1.

In any economy, concerns regarding labour, and consequently, population dynamics, have consistently constituted a fundamental policy tool, given that economic growth inherently hinges upon the interaction of capital and labour. For policymakers, the purpose of population policies is to align with and facilitate the attainment of the country's long-term development goals. In the specific case of China, its post-war population policies must be contextualized, necessitating a comprehensive assessment of policy formation, execution, and their enduring pertinence.

China's population policies are integrally interwoven with the core ideology of the ruling political party, and these ideological underpinnings, in turn, shape policymakers' comprehension of the nation's demography.

Taking the Maoist era for example: during the early years after WWII, Maoism represented the prevailing ideology within the CCP leadership. However, prior to the 1970s, China's population policies primarily revolved around the objective of stimulating fertility, aligning with the overarching tenets of Maoism that underscored the importance of a

---

jihua shengyu gongzuo de baogao (Circular of the State Council on Forwarding on the Military Control Commission of Ministry of Health, the Ministry of Commerce and the Ministry of Chemical Industry's 'Report on Better Implementing Family Planning Policy')". Beijing: The State Council of People Republic of China, 8 July 1971.

[18] Zhang, Junsen. 2017. "The Evolution of China's One-Child Policy and Its Effects on Family Outcomes." *Journal of Economic Perspectives* 31(1):141–160; Whyte, Martin King, Wang Feng, and Yong Cai. 2015. "Challenging Myths About China's One-child Policy." *The China Journal* 74:144–159.

[19] In 1973, the central government reinstated the Committee on Planned Births. Family planning efforts during the early 1970s were effectively administered through work units (*dan wei*) in urban China. This phenomenon elucidates the reason for the more rapid decline in TFR in urban areas compared to the national average during this particular period of time.

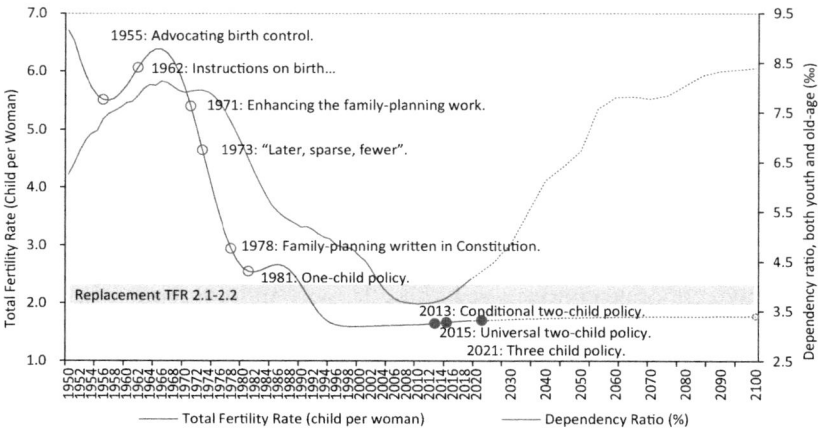

**Fig. 2.1** Total Fertility Rate and Dependency Ratio in China since 1950. (*Notes* This concept of Replacement level fertility signifies the number of children a woman must have to sustain the size of her family and, at the macro level, it represents the average reproduction rate of a population necessary to maintain the current population structure from one generation to the next. In many countries, the replacement fertility rate is estimated to be around 2.1 children per woman. This figure accounts for factors such as the preference for male new-borns and the relatively higher infant mortality rate among female infants. In developing countries, where infant mortality rates may be higher, the replacement level fertility is often slightly higher than 2.1. A commonly accepted value in academia is 2.2, considering these variations in demographic and cultural factors. *Source* National Bureau of Statistics of China. (n.d.). *Zhongguo Tongji Nianjian* (*China Statistical Yearbook*). Beijing: China Statistics Press; United Nations, Department of Economic and Social Affairs, Population Division. 2022. *World Population Prospects 2022.* Available at https://population.un.org/wpp/, accessed 15 August 2022; The World Bank. (n.d.). World Development Indicators. Washington: The World Bank. Available at https://datacatalog.worldbank.org/dataset/world-development-indicators, accessed 15 August 2023; United Nations. 2001. *World Population Ageing, 1950–2050.* https://www.un.org/development/desa/pd/sites/www.un.org.development.desa.pd/files/files/documents/2021/Nov/undesa_pd_2002_wpa_1950-2050_web.pdf, accessed 15 August 2023)

larger population base. Consequently, Mao's pro-natal policies encountered little resistance until the setbacks experienced during the Great Leap Famine.

Intra-party scepticism towards Maoism gained prominence following the failure of the Great Leap Famine, leading some of Mao's contemporaries, notably figures like Liu Shaoqi and Deng Xiaoping, to pivot towards a less-radical, Soviet-style form of socialism as opposed to adhering strictly to Maoist principles. Thus, from the 1950s through the early 1970s, the ideological divergence within the party engendered a fluctuating approach in the central government's population policy-making, oscillating between periods of "encouraging birth" and "tightening control". This oscillation was intricately linked to the dynamics of power struggle at the upper echelons of leadership. This ideological flux persisted until the late 1970s when Deng Xiaoping gradually ascended to a position of influence and embraced a transitional population policy. Subsequently, Deng adopted a fertility ideology that prioritized stringent birth control measure, marking a significant departure from the earlier emphasis on encouraging higher birth rates.

In addition to the internal disagreements among the core leadership, the central government's perception of economic growth models rooted in ideology also exerts a significant influence. In a planned economy, stiff control over resource and resource allocation was a prevailing practice seen as the ideal means to enhance economic efficiency.[20] Population, as a fundamental component of the economy, was thus considered an integral part of the planning system.[21] Within the CCP, the stance on family planning was often based on differing interpretations of Malthus's theory, as Malthusianism aligned with the foundational principles of classical economic theories upon which the CCP's growth ideology rested. Hence, even as mainstream population studies made substantial progress in the 1960s and 1970s,[22] they were not incorporated into China's

---

[20] This perspective endured even as economic reforms were initiated. Economist Liu Guoguang, a senior member of the CCP's highest decision-making body, advocated for greater central planning in the mid-1980s in order to rectify the rapid pace of economic growth that was prevalent during that period.

[21] DiMaio, Alfred J. 1980. "The Soviet Union and Population: Theory, Problems, and Population Policy." *Comparative Political Studies* 13(1):97–136.

[22] During the 1960s and 1970s, neoclassical scholars in the field were exemplified by figures such as Gary Becker and Theodore Schultz. Notable works during this period

decision-making processes. In his reform, Deng Xiaoping quickly transitioned China's growth model from one centred on agriculture to an industrial-oriented pattern, diminishing the necessity for a large population. Deng's economic shift triggered a fundamental transformation in China's population policymaking in the late 1970s.

Apart from the ideology of the top leadership, the prevailing politico-economic conditions of the era also played an important role in shaping the perspectives of policymakers regarding population. After the establishment of the PRC, the rapid post-war recovery and substantial economic support from the Soviet Union served to speed up economic growth. Thus, the set of measures implemented by the Mao government to encourage childbearing was grounded in an optimistic outlook for the nation's developmental prospects. However, this optimism began to wane in the late 1950s, as the actual economic trajectory proved to be less favourable than initially expected.

The CCP came to recognize that the rapid economic development witnessed in the 1950s was unsustainable. This realization was primarily attributed to the relatively sluggish growth of the agricultural sector, which occurred despite the swift post-war recovery. Additionally, the downturn in urban industry, a consequence of the termination of Soviet economic aid following the Sino-Soviet split,[23] contributed to this assessment. The stagnation experienced in the command economy since the mid-1960s prompted a shift in the central government's policy approach, transitioning from encouraging population growth to implementing control measures. Nonetheless, it is crucial to underscore the continued importance of ideology in this context. The alignment of policy solutions with prevailing ideology remained paramount, as any measures devised to address real economic challenges needed to be compatible with the prevailing ideological framework.

include Becker, Gary S. 1964. *Human Capital: A Theoretical and Empirical Analysis with Special Reference to Education.* New York: Columbia University Press; Schultz, Theodore W. 1963. *Economic Value of Education.* New York: Columbia University Press.

[23] The Sino-Soviet split of 1960 marked the rupture in relations between the PRC and the Soviet Union. This schism was primarily driven by a divergence in their interpretations and implementations of Marxism and Leninism, which served as the core ideological foundations of their respective Party leadership.

## The One-Child Policy and Its Bottleneck

The introduction of the "one-child policy" was primarily driven by the conflict between the state of underdevelopment[24] and the Chinese government's determination to rapidly enhance the domestic economy.[25] Before the economic reforms of 1978, China's economic structure was characterized by a predominance of agriculture and heavy industries. This economic structure, coupled with challenges such as a scarcity of arable land[26] in rural areas and the capital-intensive nature of industrial production in urban sectors, resulted in a surplus of labour within the country. China faced a confluence of factors, including a "weak economic base, huge population and low productivity".[27] Furthermore, the generation born during the baby boom of the 1950s would reach childbearing age in the mid- to late 1970s. Given this backdrop, policymakers were concerned that China might experience a new population peak, exacerbating the strain on the country's per capita capital resources.

Towards the end of the 1970s, even with the transition towards a market-based economic model, most sectors of the Chinese economy remained tightly controlled.[28] The process of de-collectivization at the early stage of marketization in the 1980s had an immediate impact on

[24] The Chinese government considered that the country's underdevelopment was largely a result of its low per capita capital stock.

[25] See, Peng, Peiyun. 1997. *Zhongguo jihua shengyu quanshu* (*A Complete Book on Chinese Family Planning*). Beijing: China Population Publishing House; Hesketh, Therese, Lu Li, and Wei Xing Zhu. 2005. "The Effect of China's One-Child Family Policy After 25 Years." *New England Journal of Medicine* 353(11):1171–1176.

[26] The per capita arable land acreage in China decreased to 1.8 *mu* in 1970 from 2.35 *mu* in 1961. Here *mu* is a unit of area measurement used in China. 40.5 mu is equivalent to 1 acre. The area of arable land per person in China was derived from data collected from the *World Development Indicators*, as sourced from The World Bank. (n.d.). World Development Indicators. Washington: The World Bank. Available at https://datacatalog. worldbank.org/dataset/world-development-indicators, accessed 15 August 2023.

[27] See the *Selected Important Documents* vol. 1., pp. 11–12. Literature Research Office of the Central Committee of Chinese Communist Party. 1982. *San zhong quanhui yilai zhongyao wenxian xuanbian* (*Selected Important Documents Since the Third Plenary Session of the 11th Central Committee of Chinese Communist Party*). Beijing: People's Publishing House.

[28] Resource allocation and wage circulation remained subject to strict state control during this period. One notable example was the urban commodity coupon system, wherein specific coupons were issued for various essential goods such as food, fabrics, and fuel.

increasing the consumption levels of the Chinese population. However, investments did not have a corresponding influence on state-controlled industrial production. This situation presented the central government with a dual challenge, referred to as the "primary contradiction" (*zhuyao maodun*), which encompassed both the excessive demand of the populace and the inadequacy of the country's output.[29] In the initial reforms of the 1980s, this economic contradiction underscored the importance of addressing the issue of population size through an intensified focus on family planning initiatives.

In this context, "family planning"[30] emerged as a basic national policy[31] as enshrined in the 1978 Constitution of the PRC.[32] The State Council, in its government report of 1980, proposed a population limit of

---

[29] In the early stage of socialism, the primary contradiction in Chinese society is characterized by the increasing material and cultural needs of the people juxtaposed with the relative underdevelopment of production capabilities.

[30] Following the release of Central Document No. 698 of 1962, the Chinese government incorporated family planning work into its Fourth Five-Year Plan (*di sige wunian jihua*) in 1971. Subsequently, in 1973, the government introduced the slogan "later, sparse, fewer" (*wan xi shao*) as a primary policy to regulate fertility. Here "later" signifies a delay in marriage and the timing of the first childbirth to a later age; "sparse" emphasizes spacing each birth interval by four to five years; and "fewer" entails limiting the total number of children for a couple to two, with no more than three as an upper limit. Further details on this policy can be found in Chinese Communist Party Central Committee, Document No. 698. 1962. "Zhonggong zhongyang guowuyuan guanyu renzhen tichang jihua shengyu de zhishi (Instruction on Earnestly Advocating Family Planning)". Beijing: Chinese Communist Party Central Committee, 18 December 1962.

[31] A similar argument can be found in the work of Schultz, T. Paul and Yi Zeng. 1995. "Fertility of Rural China. Effects of Local Family Planning and Health Programs." *Journal of Population Economics* 8(4):329–350; Attane, Isabelle. 2002. "China's Family Planning Policy: An Overview of Its Past and Future." *Studies in Family Planning* 33(1):103–113; Peng, Xizhe. 2011. "China's Demographic History and Future Challenges." *Science* 333(6042):581–587; Wang, Cuntong. 2012. "History of the Chinese Family Planning Program: 1970–2010." *Contraception* 85(6):563–569.

[32] Family planning was formally endorsed in Article No. 53 of the 1978 Constitution. This endorsement was reaffirmed and strengthened in the 1982 Constitution through Articles Nos. 25 and 49. For further reference, please see National People's Congress of People Republic of China. 1978. *Constitution of the People's Republic of China 1978*. Beijing: The First Session of the Fifth National People's Congress and Promulgated for Implementation by the Proclamation of the National People's Congress, 5 April 1978; National People's Congress of People Republic of China. 1982. *Constitution of the People's Republic of China 1982*. Beijing: The Fifth Session of the Fifth National People's Congress and Promulgated for Implementation by the Proclamation of the National People's Congress, 4 December 1978.

1.2 billion by the end of the twentieth century through the implementation of a one-child policy for all newlyweds.[33] Subsequently, in September 1980, the central government issued an *Open Letter*[34] in the *People's Daily* (*renmin rebao*) addressed to all members of CCP and the Chinese Communist Youth League (*gong qing tuan*) members concerning family planning and birth control. Within a matter of months, the stringent one-child policy was officially endorsed and incorporated into the 1981 Marriage Law.[35]

In the first decade after the implementation of the one-child policy, by the year 1990, China's birth rate declined to 2.1% (Table 2.2), with TFR stabilizing at 2.3 children per woman. However, the release of data from the third population census in late 1990 revealed that China's population was projected to reach between 1.1 to 1.2 billion, with a natural population growth rate of 1.4%. For the central government, this implied that achieving its targeted population size of below 1.2 billion by the end of twentieth century would be challenging. Hence in the Central Document

---

[33] To access specific details from the "Report on the Work of the Government 1980" delivered by Yao Yilin, one may refer to the document for more insights. See, State Council of PRC. 1980. *Report on the Work of the Government 1980*. Beijing: The Third Session of the Fifth National People's Congress and Promulgated for Implementation by the Proclamation of the National People's Congress, 30 August 1980.

[34] See, Chinese Communist Party Central Committee. 1980. "Zhonggong zhongyang guanyu kongzhi woguo renkou zengzhang wenti zhi quanti gongchan dangyuan gongqing tuanyuan de gongkaixi (The Open Letter to all CCP Members and the Chinese Youth League Members about Controls on Our Country's Population Growth)". Beijing: Renmin ribao (*People's Daily*), 25 September 1980.

[35] For more detailed information on these matters, please refer to Article No. 2, items Nos. 2 and 12 of the 1981 Marriage Law. Additionally, in a Central Document No. 13 issued in 1986, the government formally proposed the allowance for rural single-daughter families (*du nv hu*) to have an additional child. For further insights, see National People's Congress. 1980. *Marriage Law of The People's Republic of China 1981*. Beijing: The Third Session of the Fifth National People's Congress and Promulgated for Implementation by the Proclamation of the National People's Congress, 10 September 1980; Chinese Communist Party Central Committee, Document No. 13. 1986. "Zhonggong zhongyang zhuanfa guojia jishengwei guanyu 'liu wu' qijian jihua shengyu gongzuo qingkuang he 'qi wu' qijian gongzuo yijian de baogao (Circular of the Chinese Communist Party Central Committee on Forwarding 'the Report of National Family Planning Commission on the Work of Family Planning during the Sixth Five-year Plan and on the Opinion of Work during the Seventh Five-year Plan')". Beijing: Chinese Communist Party Central Committee, 9 May 1986.

No. 9 of 1991,[36] the government elevated population control to a top priority in its national plans and underscored its importance as being on par with economic growth.[37]

It was not until the late 1990s, with the improvement in industrial productivity attributed to the growth of the private sector,[38] that the primary contradiction of balancing population control with economic development began to weaken. Before this period, the contradiction had been a significant factor in the CCP's economic decision-making. Contrary to the expectation that market-oriented reforms, in the early stages of reform, China's state-led marketization model actually heightened the importance of family planning in central government's economic decision-making.

During the 1990s and 2000s, the main theme of China's population policy was the continuation and strengthening of the stringent one-child policy, with a focus on maintaining a low fertility rate.[39] Under this strict

---

[36] Chinese Communist Party Central Committee, Document No. 9. 1991. "Zhonggong zhongyang guowuyuan guanyu jiaqiang jihua shengyu gongzuo yange kongzhi renkou zengzhang de jueding (Decision of the CCP Central Committee and the State Council on Strengthening the Work of Family Planning and Strictly Controlling Population Growth)". Beijing: Chinese Communist Party Central Committee, 12 May 1991.

[37] Ibid.

[38] China's transition from state- and collectively-owned industrial enterprises to a significant presence of private enterprises began in the mid- to late 1990s. This transformation was exemplified by the emergence of Township and Village Enterprises (TVEs) in the late 1980s and 1990s. For more comprehensive insights into this economic transition, refer to Jin, Cheng. 2017. *An Economic Analysis of the Rise and Decline of Chinese Township and Village Enterprises*. Basingstoke: Palgrave Macmillan.

[39] In March 2000, the Chinese government, in its document No. 8 of that year, articulated a significant shift in its population and family planning strategy. It outlined that the primary focus of this work would transition from controlling population growth to stabilising a low fertility rate and enhancing population quality after successfully achieving fertility transition. This shift in focus was subsequently reinforced by enactment of the *Population and Family Planning Law of PRC 2001*, which came into effect in 2002. For a period spanning over a decade, the government's population policies continued to emphasize the maintenance of a low fertility rate. Central documents, such as No. 22 in 2006 and No. 39 in 2011, reiterated this priority. However, this approach saw a significant change with the conditional implementation of the two-child policies since 2013, signifying the end of the stringent one-child policy that had been in place for three decades. For more detailed information and references to specific documents and decrees related to these policy changes, one can refer to Information Office of the State Council of PRC. 2000. "Zhongguo 21 shiji renkou yu fazhan (China's Population and

**Table 2.2**   China's population during the one-child policy

| Year | Birth rate (‰) | Mortality rate (‰) | Natural increase rate (‰) | Total population (Million persons) (‰) |
|------|------|------|------|------|
| (1) | (2) | (3) | (4) | (5) |
| 1980 | 18.2 | 6.3 | 11.9 | 1127.0 |
| 1981 | 20.9 | 6.4 | 14.6 | 1143.3 |
| 1982 | 22.3 | 6.6 | 15.7 | 1158.2 |
| 1983 | 20.2 | 6.9 | 13.3 | 1171.7 |
| 1984 | 19.9 | 6.8 | 13.1 | 1185.2 |
| 1985 | 21.0 | 6.8 | 14.3 | 1198.5 |
| 1986 | 22.4 | 6.9 | 15.6 | 1211.2 |
| 1987 | 23.3 | 6.7 | 16.6 | 1223.9 |
| 1988 | 22.4 | 6.6 | 15.7 | 1236.3 |
| 1989 | 21.6 | 6.5 | 15.0 | 1247.6 |
| 1990 | 21.1 | 6.7 | 14.4 | 1257.9 |
| 1991 | 19.7 | 6.7 | 13.0 | 1267.4 |
| 1992 | 18.2 | 6.6 | 11.6 | 1276.3 |
| 1993 | 18.1 | 6.6 | 11.5 | 1284.5 |
| 1994 | 17.7 | 6.5 | 11.2 | 1292.3 |
| 1995 | 17.1 | 6.6 | 10.6 | 1299.9 |
| 1996 | 17.0 | 6.6 | 10.4 | 1307.6 |
| 1997 | 16.6 | 6.5 | 10.1 | 1314.5 |
| 1998 | 15.6 | 6.5 | 9.1 | 1321.3 |
| 1999 | 14.6 | 6.5 | 8.2 | 1328.0 |
| 2000 | 14.0 | 6.5 | 7.6 | 1334.5 |
| 2001 | 13.4 | 6.4 | 7.0 | 1340.9 |
| 2002 | 12.9 | 6.4 | 6.5 | 1349.2 |
| 2003 | 12.4 | 6.4 | 6.0 | 1359.2 |
| 2004 | 12.3 | 6.4 | 5.9 | 1367.3 |
| 2005 | 12.4 | 6.5 | 5.9 | 1127.0 |
| 2006 | 12.1 | 6.8 | 5.3 | 1143.3 |
| 2007 | 12.1 | 6.9 | 5.2 | 1158.2 |
| 2008 | 12.1 | 7.1 | 5.1 | 1171.7 |
| 2009 | 12.0 | 7.1 | 4.9 | 1185.2 |
| 2010 | 11.9 | 7.1 | 4.8 | 1198.5 |
| 2011 | 11.9 | 7.1 | 4.8 | 1211.2 |
| 2012 | 12.1 | 7.2 | 5.0 | 1223.9 |
| 2013 | 12.1 | 7.2 | 4.9 | 1236.3 |

*Source* National Bureau of Statistics of China. (n.d.). *Zhongguo Tongji Nianjian* (*China Statistical Yearbook*). Beijing: China Statistics Press

family planning policy, China experienced a continuous decline in its birth rate, decreasing from 2.1% in 1990 to 1.2% in 2010. Additionally, the natural population growth rate also saw a substantial drop, falling from 1.4% to 0.5% during the same period (as indicated in Table 2.2). By 2010, China's TFR had fallen to 1.6, significantly below the replacement level. This trend underscored the effectiveness of the one-child policy in controlling population growth, but it also raised concerns about demographic challenges, including an ageing population and potential labour force shortages.

## The Reversal of Population Control Policies

China's rapid economic growth has benefited from historical demographic trends. The high birth rate in the 1960s and 1970s, coupled with the subsequent restrictive birth policies implemented in the 1980s, created a favourable demographic situation. These policies reduced child dependency pressure and allowed the redirection of social resources towards manufacturing and production, hence facilitating fast industrialization and economic growth. However, it is important to note that this demographic advantage has limitations and is likely to be a short-term effect.

Development in the 21st Century)." *White Paper of the Government of PRC*. Beijing: Information Office of the State Council of the People's Republic of China, December 2000; Chinese Communist Party Central Committee, Document No. 8. 2000. "Zhonggong zhongyang guowuyuan guanyu jiaqiang renkou yu jihua shengyu gongzuo wending di shengyu shuiping de jueding (Decision of the CCP Central Committee and the State Council on 'Strengthening the Work of Population and Family Planning and Stabilising Low Fertility Level')". Beijing: Chinese Communist Party Central Committee, 2 March 2000; National People's Congress. 2001. *Population and Family Planning Law of the People's Republic of China 2002*. Beijing: The Twenty-fifth Session of Standing Committee of the Ninth National People's Congress and Promulgated for Implementation by the Proclamation of the National People's Congress, 29 December 2001; Chinese Communist Party Central Committee, Document No. 22. 2006. "Zhonggong zhongyang guowuyuan guanyu quanmian jiaqiang renkou he jihua shengyu gongzuo tongchou jiejue renkou wenti de jueding (Decision of the Central Committee of the CCP Central Committee and the State Council on 'Comprehensively Strengthening of Population and Family Planning Work and Solving the Population Problem')". Beijing: Chinese Communist Party Central Committee, 17 December 2006; State Council of People's Republic of China, Document No. 39. 2011. "Guowuyuan guanyu yinfa guojia renkou fazhan 'shi er wu' guihua de tongzhi (Circular of the State Council on Printing and Issuing 'the National "12th Five-Year Plan" for Population Development')". Beijing: The State Council of People's Republic of China, 23 November 2011.

The transition from high birth rates in the 1960s to low birth rates in the 2010s and 2020s represents a continuous release of labour stock that was saved before the 1970s.[40] This demographic change has provided a temporary boost to the labour force without a corresponding accumulation of labour resources afterwards.

The robust economic growth experienced in the post-reform era has been significantly fuelled by a plentiful labour supply, primarily from individuals born in the 1950s and 1960s. However, the rapidly declining birth rate in subsequent decades implies a looming labour shortage in China's current and future labour market. This shortage could have adverse implications for both economic growth and income transition.[41] By the end of the 2020s, people born in the 1960s reach their 60s, marking the typical retirement age. As these large cohorts exit the labour market, the deep decline in the TFR and birth rate between the 1960s and 1980s, as depicted in Fig. 2.1, will further exacerbate the challenge of maintaining an adequate labour supply in China. The inadequacy of necessary labour supply seems increasingly imminent and is likely to present significant hurdles for sustaining economic growth.

The data from the 2022 sample population survey indicate that China's total dependency ratio has reached 46.6%,[42] which means about 47 elderly and young individuals for every 100 working-age individuals who rely on them for care and support. The same ratio is expected to rise significantly to 63.9% by the year 2050 (Table 2.3),[43] suggesting that

[40] The decline in China's TFR from a high of 4.5 in 1960 to 1.2 in 2021 is a significant demographic shift and reflects the long-term impact of population control policies, primarily the one-child policy and its subsequent iterations. For detailed data, please refer to The World Bank. (n.d.). World Development Indicators. Washington: The World Bank. Available at https://datacatalog.worldbank.org/dataset/world-development-indicators, accessed 15 August 2023.

[41] China's transition from the lower-income to upper-middle-income category in 2009, according to the World Bank, signifies a significant milestone in its economic development.

[42] The total dependency ratio in China, as of 2022, is calculated by combining both the elderly dependency ratio, which stands at 21.8%, and the child dependency ratio, which is 24.8%. These figures are based on sample population survey data collected from National Bureau of Statistics of China. (n.d.). National Data. Available at https://data.stats.gov.cn/english/easyquery.htm?cn=C01, accessed 15 August 2023.

[43] Population projection data are collected from United Nations. For detailed data, refer to United Nations. 2001. "World Population Ageing, 1950–2050." Available at

nearly two-thirds of the Chinese population will require care and support at that time.[44]

**Table 2.3**  Structure of Chinese population after 1950

| | 1950 (1) | 1975 (2) | 2000 (3) | 2025 (4) | 2050 (5) |
|---|---|---|---|---|---|
| Age 0–14 [Million Persons] | 186.0 | 366.4 | 316.8 | 269.9 | 238.4 |
| _Percentage Share of Total Population (%) | [33.5%] | [39.5%] | [24.8%] | [18.4%] | [16.3%] |
| Age 15–64 [Million Persons] | 343.9 | 520.6 | 870.9 | 1006.1 | 892.0 |
| _Percentage Share of Total Population (%) | [62.0%] | [56.1%] | [68.3%] | [68.4%] | [61.0%] |
| Age 65 + [Million Persons] | 24.9 | 40.8 | 86.5 | 194.0 | 331.1 |
| _Percentage Share of Total Population (%) | [4.5%] | [4.4%] | [6.8%] | [13.2%] | [22.6%] |
| Median Age (Years) | 23.9 | 20.6 | 30.0 | 39.0 | 43.8 |
| Dependency Ratio _Total (%) | 61.3 | 78.2 | 46.4 | 46.2 | 63.9 |
| _Youth (%) | 54.1 | 70.4 | 36.4 | 26.8 | 26.7 |
| _Old Age (%) | 7.2 | 7.8 | 10.0 | 19.4 | 37.2 |
| Potential Support Ratio | 13.8 | 12.8 | 10.0 | 5.2 | 2.7 |

*Notes* The potential support ratio is a demographic indicator that specifically focuses on the burden of the non-working elderly population on the working-age population. Unlike the dependency ratio, which includes both the elderly and children, the potential support ratio excludes consideration of the unemployed and children. It provides insight into the relative balance between the working-age population and the elderly population in terms of the potential support and care they can provide to the elderly. A declining potential support ratio often reflects an ageing population and can have implications for social welfare, healthcare, and pension systems

*Source* National Bureau of Statistics of China. (n.d.). *Zhongguo Tongji Nianjian* (China Statistical Yearbook). Beijing: China Statistics Press; United Nations. 2001. "World Population Ageing, 1950–2050". Available at    https://www.un.org/development/desa/pd/sites/www.un.org.development. desa.pd/files/files/documents/2021/Nov/undesa_pd_2002_wpa_1950-2050_web.pdf , accessed 15 August 2023

https://www.un.org/development/desa/pd/sites/www.un.org.development.desa.pd/ files/files/documents/2021/Nov/undesa_pd_2002_wpa_1950-2050_web.pdf,    accessed 15 August 2023.

[44] In accordance with a global population survey conducted by the United Nations, it is projected that by the year 2050, the Chinese population aged over 60 years will reach a total of 437.0 million, constituting approximately 29.9% of China's total population. For additional details, please refer to the United Nations. 2001. "World Population Ageing, 1950–2050". Available at https://www.un.org/development/desa/pd/sites/ www.un.org.development.desa.pd/files/files/documents/2021/Nov/undesa_pd_2002_ wpa_1950-2050_web.pdf, accessed 15 August 2023.

Nevertheless, China's demographic change is projected to exacerbate further, with the potential support ratio declining from 12.8 in 1975 to a mere 2.7 by 2050. Concurrently, the elderly population (those aged 65 and older) is estimated to surge from 40.8 million in 1950 to 331.1 million in 2050, constituting approximately one-quarter of the total population. This implies that a substantial portion of China's population will be in retirement and will have exited the labour market by then.

The percentage of the working-age population, defined as individuals aged 15–64, is expected to decline by over seven percentage points from 68.3–68.4 in 2000–2025 to 61.0% in 2050 (as indicated in Table 2.2). Meanwhile, between 2010 and 2050, China's labour force is expected to contract by 250 million, leading to an overall reduction in the size of the effective labour supply to levels comparable to those seen in 1975.

The labour shrinkage, in the context of a fourfold increase in the elderly population, is poised to have significant implications. As depicted in Fig. 2.2, while the youth dependency ratio has stabilized since 2010, the elderly dependency ratio has started to surge. The net outcome of these demographic changes, represented by the potential dependency ratio, reveals that by the year 2050, each elderly individual in China will rely on the support of only 2.7 working-age individuals, not taking into account the number of children under the care of the working-age group.

When compounded by the effects of increased life expectancy and a rise in the average wage level, attributed to four decades of rapid economic growth, the monetary support ratio provided by the working-age population will become even more significant than the projected 2.7 in 2050. This implies that the working-age generation will be required to contribute more substantially to social welfare and support systems in order to sustain the growing elderly population.

Alongside adequate capital accumulation, labour supply serves as the backbone of China's economic transition, effectively charting the course for the country's economic future. Though the Chinese government had fundamentally revised its population policies since 2013, which now permit parents to have up to three children, these measures alone may prove insufficient to counteract the trajectory of a substantial decline in the proportion of China's working-age population.

While the relaxation of birth restrictions has indeed provided families with the opportunity to have more children, several factors, including the long-standing history of birth restrictions and the rapid escalation of

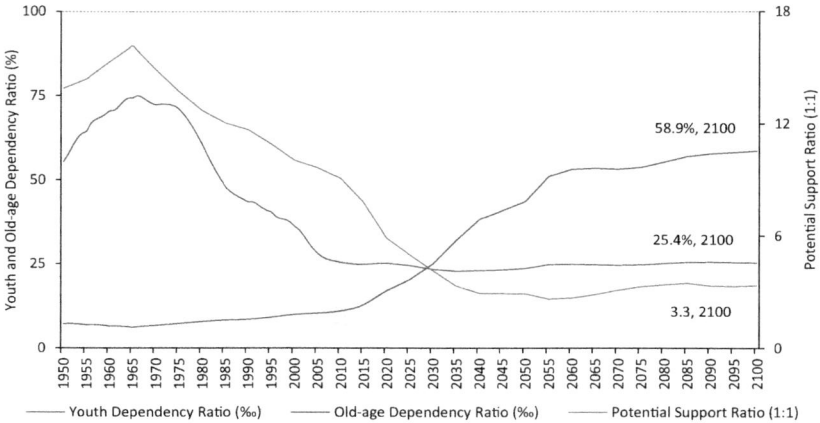

**Fig. 2.2** Estimated Dependency Ratio and Potential Support Ratio of China (*Source* United Nations, Department of Economic and Social Affairs, Population Division. 2022. *World Population Prospects 2022*. Available at https://popula tion.un.org/wpp/ , accessed 15 August 2023)

living costs, continue to influence Chinese people's decisions regarding additional children. Although there were two minor upticks in birth rates following the easing of the one-child policy, these increases were short-lived and were followed by a rapid decline. These trends suggest that the impact of relaxing the one-child policy has been rather limited, and the broader demographic trajectory in China is not expected to reverse significantly.

While some Chinese demography experts estimated that the relaxation of the one-child policy would lead to a modest increase of one to two million births from 2013 to 2016, this estimation is now considered overly optimistic. Even if the general fertility rate[45] had indeed experienced a successful increase, it would still take nearly two decades for the effects of the eased one-child policy to become apparent in terms of the country's dependency ratios and labour supply.

The relaxation of the one-child policy has thus far not yielded the expected results, let alone narrowed the gap between future labour demand and supply. Despite the implementation of current population easing policies, it is projected that from 2025 to 2050, the workforce in China will still experience a significant decline of 11.3% (as indicated in Table 2.3). This decline constitutes an unprecedented labour contraction in human history.[46]

This aligns with the ongoing trend of a declining total population size. It is evident that the present population policies, including the recently introduced three-child policy, fall short in alleviating the future labour market pressures in China. While the relaxation of the one-child policy represents a significant step forward, there remains a pressing need for more intensive and proactive population policies aimed at bolstering fertility rates. Such measures are essential to counteract the ongoing decline in the workforce and its associated challenges.

## Two-Sided Effects of the One-Child Policy

From 1980 to 2013, the one-child rule imposed significant limitations on most Chinese families, restricting them to having only one child each. Over the course of more than three decades of this policy, it became deeply ingrained as a social norm in Chinese society. By the end of the

[45] The general fertility rate is a comprehensive metric used to gauge fertility in a population. It quantifies the total number of live births per 1,000 women within the childbearing age range in a given population over the course of a year. This measurement is regarded as a more refined approach to assessing fertility compared to traditional birth rates and the TFR. The distinction lies in the fact that the general fertility rate focuses exclusively on the female population aged 15–44 years when calculating the denominator, as opposed to considering the entire population. By doing so, it provides a more accurate representation of potential fertility behaviour while also factoring in age distribution. This sets it apart from the TFR, which does not incorporate age distribution into its calculations.

[46] Before the implementation of China's population easing policies, from 1990 to 2013, Russia faced a depopulation challenge, often referred to as a "depopulation bomb". During this period, Russia experienced one of the fastest declines in its working-age population in modern history, with a decrease of only 10.2%.

2000s, the Chinese government officially claimed that as many as 400 million births had been prevented due to the country's stringent birth restriction policies.[47]

In the immediate aftermath of the one-child rule, there was a rapid decrease in the number of new-borns during the 1980s and 1990s, while improved living standard helped increase Chinese people's longevity.[48] The combined effect of these demographic changes was a notable improvement in the structure of workforce in the total Chinese population.

Figure 2.3 offers a comparative analysis of China's working-age structure in relation to all other income categories, revealing three distinct features in China's working-age structure:

- A sudden increase in the early 1980s;
- A substantially higher peak level in comparison to all income groups; and
- A notable and sharp reversal in the first half of the 2010s.

Reflective of reality at the time:

- The implementation of China's one-child rule had a rapid effect on making the country's overall demographics younger;
- As a result, it propelled China's labour supply on an upward trajectory before 2010;
- And it condensed China's demographic transition within the relatively short timeframe of 1980 to 2050.

This concentrated demographic changes firmly supported China's economic take-off and income transition in the past four decades:

---

[47] National Bureau of Statistics. 2009. Xin Zhongguo chengli 60 zhounian xilie baogao zhiwu: renkou zongliang shidu zengzhang jiegou mingxian gaishan (New China 60th Anniversary Report Series No. 5: Moderate Increase in Total Population and Significant Improvement in Its Structure). Available at https://www.gov.cn/test/2009-09/15/con tent_1417725.htm, accessed 15 August 2023.

[48] For detailed studies on the impact of China's demographic changes on its export-led growth model, please refer to Yao, Yang. 2011. "The Relationship between China's Export-led Growth and Its Double Transition of Demographic Change and Industrialization." *Asian Economic Papers* 10(2):52–76.

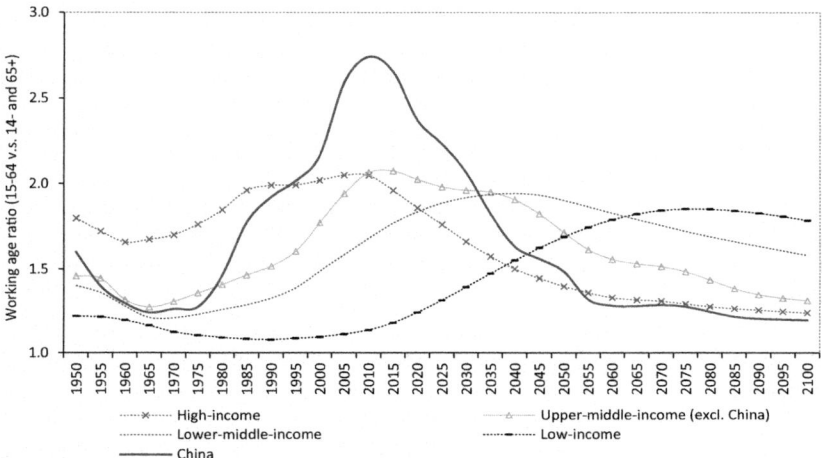

**Fig. 2.3** Working-age ratios, China among all income groups (*Note* The working-age ratio is a demographic indicator that assesses the structure of the productive population. It is calculated as the ratio of individuals within the labour force [typically aged 15–64] to those not in the labour force [usually aged 14 and younger, as well as 64 and older]. This ratio serves as a key metric for understanding the composition of the population in terms of its ability to contribute to the workforce and overall productivity. For geographic comparison of working-age structure between China and other regions of the world, please refer to Yao, Yang. 2011. "The Relationship between China's Export-led Growth and Its Double Transition of Demographic Change and Industrialization." *Asian Economic Papers* 10(2): 52–76. *Source* United Nations, Department of Economic and Social Affairs, Population Division. 2022. World Population Prospects 2022. Available at https://population.un.org/wpp/ , accessed 15 August 2023)

- From the mid-1980s to the late 1990s, the presence of a substantial labour force facilitated the country's initial phase of industrialization;
- Subsequently, the sufficient labour supply supported China's industrial privatization since the late 1990s, bolstering export-led economic growth;

- And later this labour force was leveraged as a comparative advantage, particularly in terms of "low wage cost", contributing significantly to China's performance in the World Trade Organisation (WTO).[49]

The simultaneous implementation of the one-child policy with China's economic opening up has led many to associate the country's rapid economic and social transformations with this policy.[50] Some have suggested that population control measures effectively alleviated social dependency pressures and contributed to the rapid accumulation of a young labour force. This labour force, in turn, provided China's productive sectors, particularly the industrial sector, with a sustainable influx of low-cost labour, which greatly supported the country's fast economic transition.

It was also argued that the one-child policy generated privileged generations,[51] particularly beneficial for China's economic transition in the 2000s when the first generation born under this policy became a key demographic group within Chinese society. These assertions highlight the complex relationship between population policies and China's economic development, acknowledging the multifaceted impacts of such policies on the country's demographic structure and labour dynamics.

However, the negative side is that the positive outcomes of the policy primarily manifested as short-term effects. In the long term, the elevation of income levels[52] was observed to diminish people's desire for

[49] In a comparative analysis among East Asian countries and major processing trade nations in Southeast Asia, China stands out for having one of the cheapest labour forces working in the manufacturing sector, as reported by the Conference Board. This cost advantage persisted even after the investment boom of 2008, with China's labour costs continuing to rank among the lower-wage countries in Asia. For further details, please refer to the Conference Board. 2016. International Comparisons of Hourly Compensation Costs in Manufacturing and Sub-Manufacturing Industries. Available at https://www.conference-board.org/retrievefile.cfm?filename=ilccompensationtimeseries_2016.xlsx, accessed 15 August 2023.

[50] For example, Wang, Feng, and Andrew Mason. 2008. "The Demographic Factor in China's Transition." In Brandt, Loren, and Thomas G. Rawski (eds.). *China's Great Economic Transformation*. Cambridge: Cambridge University Press, pp. 136–166.

[51] Heckman, James J. 2005. "China's Human Capital Investment." *China Economic Review* 16(1):50–70.

[52] Neoclassical economic theories contend that the decline in birth rates and fertility desires is an inherent feature of economic growth, particularly when income and education levels are elevated due to improved living standards. This perspective aligns with the ideas

fertility.[53] Furthermore, China's one-child policy has exacerbated this declining birth trend. Thus, the Chinese population has been rapidly aging, particularly as the first generation born under the one-child policy reached childbearing age during the 2000s and 2010s. This rapid decline in the working-age population will not only lead to social challenges, such as pension deficits, but will also directly lead to a rapid elevation in industrial wage levels.

## RISING WAGE EFFECTS OF DEMOGRAPHIC SHIFTS

The stringent implementation of family planning measures ensured a sufficient labour force during the initial two to three decades of reform, characterized by a favourable demographic composition contributed significantly to China's unprecedented growth and expeditious industrialization. With the implementation of the one-child rule, China started its modern population transition.

A conceptual framework that aids in comprehending the repercussions of shifts in population structure on the tangible economy could be encapsulated in the notion of a critical juncture wherein the labour supply diminishes below the concurrent industrial demand—commonly referred to as the Lewis turning point.[54]

While data from the National Bureau of Statistics indicate that the decline in working-age population (aged 15 to 64) only commenced

---

put forth by Gary S. Becker in his work in 1964. Refer to Becker, Gary S. 1964. *Human Capital: A Theoretical and Empirical Analysis with Special Reference to Education.* New York: Columbia University Press.

[53] For a neoclassical perspective on China's situation, one can refer to Cai, Fang. 2010. "Demographic Transition, Demographic Dividend, and Lewis Turning Point in China." *China Economic Journal* 3(2):107–119; McElroy, Marjorie and Dennis Tao Yang. 2000. "Carrots and Sticks: Fertility Effects of China's Population Policies." *The American Economic Review* 90(2):389–392.

[54] The Lewis turning point delineates a concept in economic advancement characterised by the complete absorption of surplus labour from rural regions and/or the agricultural sector into the secondary industrial sector. This transition commonly gives rise to an escalation in wages across both the agricultural and unskilled industrial domains. This concept was originally introduced by William Arthur Lewis in 1972. See, Lewis, William Arthur. 1972. "Reflections on Unlimited Labour." In Di Marco, Luis Eugenio (ed.). *International Economics and Development: Essays in Hornor of Raul Prebisch.* New York: Elsevier, pp. 75–96.

in 2013–2014,[55] in fact, the labour market reversal in fact happened a decade earlier in 2005.[56] The transformation in China's population structure attributable to reduced fertility rates is discernible in both the overall age distribution and the demographic composition of the working-age populace, both of which are experiencing profound changes consequent to the enforcement of the one-child policy.

When concerns arose on China's Lewis turning point due to changes in population structure, a notable transformation resulting from the constricted labour market was the rapid escalation in the wages of the workforce. Currently, the trajectory of wage income and wage rates in the Chinese population has undergone two distinct phases of development.

- Before 1980, the central planning system rendered rural labour surplus in the agriculture, a condition that persisted until Deng's reform liberated China's labour distribution, facilitating intersectoral and interregional labour mobility. The increased participation of labour in urban industries significantly contributed to the growth of income in the Chinese population until the labour market reached its threshold in 2004–2005. The abundance of rural labour supply, on the one hand, kept industrial wage rates consistently low; on the other hand, it accentuated China's comparative advantages in labour-intensive industries after reform. During the 1980s and 1990s, the substantial increase in the participation of agricultural workforce in both rural (e.g. TVEs) and urban industries rapidly elevated Chinese income levels. From 1990 to 2004, the annual addition of rural

---

[55] The aggregate count of the working-age population, ranging from 15 to 64 years old, as estimated by the United Nations, witnessed a decline from 1014.0 million persons in 2019 to 1012.1 million in 2020. In contrast, official data from China's National Bureau of Statistics reveal that this demographic cohort reached its zenith at 1010.4 million persons in 2013, initiating a descent to 1010.3 million in 2014. Notably, this decline commenced six years earlier than the corresponding estimate provided by the United Nations. For specific details, please refer to United Nations, Department of Economic and Social Affairs, Population Division. 2022. World Population Prospects 2022. Available at https://population.un.org/wpp/, accessed 15 August 2023; National Bureau of Statistics. (n.d.). *National Data*. Available at https://data.stats.gov.cn/index.htm, accessed 15 August 2023.

[56] There are other scholars who have computed this turning point occurred in 2004. See, Cai, Fang. 2010. "Demographic Transition, Demographic Dividend, and Lewis Turning Point in China." *China Economic Journal* 3(2):107–119.

migrant workers surged from 1.8 million to a peak of 13.9 million[57]; meanwhile, the share with wage income in rural household net income rose from 20.2% to 32.4% during the same period.

- Following the turning point in 2004–2005, the reversed supply-demand relationship in the labour market significantly increased China's industrial wage rates (refer to Fig. 2.4). From 2004 to 2012, average wage rates for rural migrant workers increased at an annual rate of 14.4%.[58] However, this fast increase in wage rates augmented industrial production costs, thereby weakening China's comparative advantage of low labour cost in global competitiveness.

Following the substantial increase in 2004–2005, the trajectory of increasing wage rates experienced an accelerated upward momentum in the 2010s (refer to Fig. 2.4), suggesting that China's labour supply may have neared its upper threshold.[59] This discernment is reinforced by data from the National Bureau of Statistics, shown in Table 2.4, where the size of the rural migrant workers has exhibited a stagnation since 2013. This stagnation provides supplementary evidence of China's diminishing demographic dividend.

Undoubtedly, the immediate impact of the one-child policy was the mitigation of childbearing responsibilities and youth dependency among China's young working ages, providing firm support for the rapid industrialization witnessed in the 1980s and 1990s. However, as the demographic dividend gradually dissipated in the mid-2010s, both the size and proportion of working-age population started to decline as quickly as they had ascended. This structural deterioration in demographics is expected

---

[57] Data of Chinese migrant workers were collected from the work of Lu, Feng. 2011. "Zhongguo nongaming gong gongzi dingliang guce 1979–2010 (Quantitative Estimation of Wage Rates for Chinese Migrant Workers 1979–2010)." *China Centre for Economic Research Working Paper Series* No. C2011020. Published on 18 November 2011. Available at https://nsd.pku.edu.cn/pub/chnsd/attachments/6548c6f9e6314a4fb20a4efdec5ff4a2.pdf, accessed 15 August 2023.

[58] Since 2014, wage rates for migrant workers started to decelerate.

[59] While the reverse of labour demand and supply happened in the mid-2000s, the absolute number of the working-age population in China began to decrease during the 2010s and is expected to continue on its downward trajectory until the first generation born under the one-child policy reaches their retirement ages in the 2040s. Data are sourced from OECD. (n.d.). Historical population data and projections (1950–2050). Available at https://stats.oecd.org/index.aspx?DataSetCode=POP_PROJ, accessed 15 August 2023.

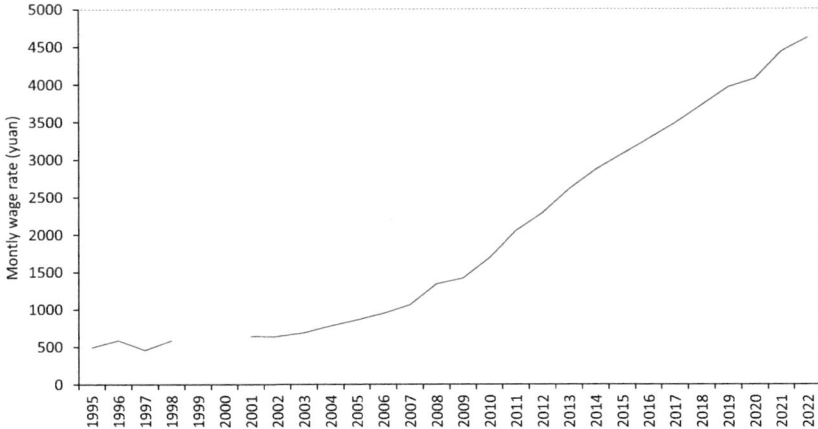

**Fig. 2.4** Monthly wage rates for migrant workers, 1995–2022 (*Note* 1995–2007 wage rates for migrant workers were collected from Lu [2011]. 2008–2022 data were from annual Migrant Workers' Monitoring Survey Reports and National Bureau of Statistics' National Data. *Source* Lu, Feng. 2011. "Zhongguo nongaming gong gongzi dingliang guce 1979–2010 (Quantitative Estimation of Wage Rates for Chinese Migrant Workers 1979–2010)". China Centre for Economic Research Working Paper Series No. C2011020. Published on 18 November 2011. Available at https://nsd.pku.edu.cn/pub/chnsd/attachments/6548c6f9e6314a4fb20a4efdec5ff4a2.pdf, accessed 15 August 2023; National Bureau of Statistics of China. 2010. Migrant Workers Monitoring Survey Report 2009. Available at http://cn.chinagate.cn/reports/2010-03/22/content_19655996_3.htm, accessed 15 August 2023; National Bureau of Statistics of China. 2023. Migrant Workers Monitoring Survey Report 2022. Available at http://www.stats.gov.cn/sj/zxfb/202304/t20230427_1939124.html, accessed 15 August 2023; National Bureau of Statistics. (n.d.). National Data. Available at https://data.stats.gov.cn/index.htm, accessed 15 August 2023)

to persist until the first generation born under the one-child policy reaches retirement ages in the 2040s and 2050s, as discussed in Fig. 2.3.

Moreover, this decline in the working-age population is poised to instigate not only challenges related to ageing and pension deficits,[60] but also impediments in terms of labour-constrained economic growth

[60] Bloom, David E., David Canning, and Günther Fink. 2010. "Implications of Population Ageing for Economic Growth." *Oxford Review of Economic Policy* 26(4):583–612.

**Table 2.4** Size of migrant workers since China upgraded to upper-middle-income in 2009

| Year (1) | Size of Migrant Workers (Million persons) (2) | Annual growth rate (Percentage point %) (3) |
|---|---|---|
| 2009 | 229.8 | – |
| 2010 | 242.2 | 5.4 |
| 2011 | 252.8 | 4.4 |
| 2012 | 262.6 | 3.9 |
| 2013 | 268.9 | 2.4 |
| 2014 | 274.0 | 1.9 |
| 2015 | 277.5 | 1.3 |
| 2016 | 281.7 | 1.5 |
| 2017 | 286.5 | 1.7 |
| 2018 | 288.4 | 0.6 |
| 2019 | 290.8 | 0.8 |
| 2020 | 285.6 | −1.8 |
| 2021 | 292.5 | 2.4 |
| 2022 | 295.6 | 1.1 |

*Source* National Bureau of Statistics of China. 2023. *Migrant Workers Monitoring Survey Report 2022.* Available at http://www.stats.gov.cn/sj/zxfb/202304/t20230427_1939124.html, accessed 15 August 2023; National Bureau of Statistics of China. 2018. *Migrant Workers Monitoring Survey Report 2017.* Available at https://app.www.gov.cn/govdata/gov/201804/28/423387/article.html, accessed 15 August 2023; National Bureau of Statistics of China. 2013. *Migrant Workers Monitoring Survey Report 2012.* Available at https://www.gov.cn/gzdt/2013-05/27/content_2411923.htm, accessed 15 August 2023

path. Consequently, as China's labour market surpassed its thresholds of Lewis turning and demographic dividend,[61] the nation is compelled to confront increasing difficulties in sourcing adequate workforces to sustain its ongoing transition.

Weil, David N. 1997. "The Economics of Population Aging." *Handbook of Population and Family Economics* 1(B):967–1014.

[61] Detailed discussion about China's Lewis turning point and the disappearing of demographic dividend in China would be found in Chapter 3.

# FROM FAMILY PLANNING TO BIRTH ENCOURAGING POLICIES

Unlike other economic policies, population policy has its own constraints: the effect of a change in fertility rates takes a generation to be evident in the labour market, and reversing its effect may come too late. This lag in the effectiveness of population policies presents challenges for decision-makers in assessing their future outcomes.

While it is not difficult to predict demographic changes (e.g. population size and structure) brought about by some specific population policies such as delivering the central's policy goals of reducing population, the real difficulty lies in determining whether the initial rationale for implementing such a policy remains valid 15 to 20 years down the line. In practice, changes in the core leadership of the CCP and evolving socio-economic conditions have rendered the population policies of the 1960s obsolete, as they are no longer aligned with, and may even contradict, China's economic requirements before the year 2010.

The three-decade-long implementation of the one-child rule in China effectively reduced the country's population size. However, the majority of this reduction occurred within the younger age groups. When the first generation born under the one-child policy reached marriage and child-bearing age, China's population structure began to undergo a reversal. The Chinese government adopted a set of expansionary policies to mitigate external influences from the post-2008 global economic recession, the rapid growth of the Chinese economy and the resulting high demand for labour have intensified labour market pressure.

A notable consequence of these policies was the rapid increase in the selection ratio in China's labour market. This abrupt rise in labour demand ultimately marked a turning point in China's labour market in the 2010s: China's working-age population shifted from an excess of labour supply to a tight supply–demand balance, and gradually to continuous labour shortage thereafter. China is now seen as a country facing a pronounced labour shortage.[62]

---

[62] The selection ratio is a term that refers to the ratio of the number of job positions available to the number of job applicants seeking those positions. For a more detailed discussion and similar arguments, one can refer to the work of Cai, Fang. 2008. *Liuyisi zhuanzhedian:zhongguo jingji fazhan xin jieduan* (*Lewis Turning Point: A Coming New Stage of Chinas Economic Development*). Beijing: Social Sciences Academic Press; Li, Daokiu and Xiang Xu. 2012. *Zhongguo renkou yu laodong wenti baogao No. 13:*

Low birth rates and rapid population ageing[63] have fundamentally changed China's population structure and labour market dynamics. Calls for the government to relax population control policies[64] have emerged as concerns over labour shortages intensify. Since the early 2010s, the Chinese government has demonstrated a willingness to gradually ease birth control measures. After the release of Central Document No. 12 by the CCP Central Committee in 2013,[65] China initiated a shift away from the one-child policy, introducing the "conditional two-child policy",[66] which permitted parents who were themselves the only child to have a second child.

However, this relaxation of population control policies had limited success in stimulating higher birth rates: In the years 2013, 2014, and 2015, birth rates remained low at 12.1‰, 12.4‰, and 12.1‰, respectively. Evidently, other factors are influencing individuals' decisions to forgo having additional children, suggesting that more robust measures may be necessary.[67]

---

*renkou zhuanbian yu zhongguo jingji zai pingheng* (*Reports on China's Population and Labour No. 13: Demographic Transition and Economic Rebalance in China*). Beijing: Social Sciences Academic Press; Wang, Fei, Liqiu Zhao, Zhong Zhao. 2017. "China's Family Planning Policies and Their Labor Market Consequences." *Journal of Population Economics* 30(1):31–68.

[63] While the TFR experienced a significant decline from 6.4 in 1965 to 1.6 in 2009, a period during which China achieved upper-middle-income status, the nation's old-age dependency ratio concurrently increased substantially from 6.2% to 11.0%.

[64] For example, Lin, Justin Yifu. 2013. *Shengyu zhengce tiaozheng yu zhongguo fazhan* (*Fertility Policy Adjustment and Development in China*). Beijing: Social Sciences Academic Press.

[65] Chinese Communist Party Central Committee, Document No. 12. 2013. "Zhonggong zhongyang guanyu quanmian shenhua gaige ruogan zhongda wenti de jueding (Decision of the CCP Central Committee on Some Major Issues Concerning Comprehensively Deepening the Reform)". Beijing: The Third Session of the Eighteenth Central Committee of the Chinese Communist Party, 12 November 2013.

[66] The detailed implementation rules for the conditional two-child policy were promptly outlined in Central Document No. 15 of 2013. See, Chinese Communist Party Central Committee, Document No. 15. 2013. "Zhonggong zhongyang guowuyuan yinfa guanyu tiaozheng wanshan shengyu zhengce de yijian (Opinions Issued by the CCP Central Committee and the State Council on 'Adjusting and Improving the Family Planning Policy')". Beijing: 30 December 2013.

[67] Liu, Haoming. 2014. "The Quality–Quantity Trade-off: Evidence from the Relaxation of China's One-Child Policy." *Journal of Population Economics* 27(2):565–602.

Consequently, in 2015, the Chinese government removed this condition, granting all couples the choice to have two children in its document No. 40 issued in 2015.[68] In the "National Plan for Population Development (2016–2030)" published in 2016,[69] the government clearly emphasized the risk posed by a low fertility rate to the country and positioned its new policy of "a balanced population development" (*renkou junheng fazhan*) among national strategies. After the implementation of the "universal two-child policy", China's birth rate rebounded to 13.0‰ in 2016, with the TFR experiencing a slight increase from 1.6 in 2010 to 1.7 in 2016.

Hence, in 2021, the Chinese government further relaxed its fertility control measures, introducing the "three-child policy", which allows couples to have up to three children,[70] marking another significant amendment to population policy. Nevertheless, China's TFR remains considerably lower than the 2.1–2.2 replacement level necessary for maintaining and balancing the country's current demographic equilibrium.

In China, the formulation of social and economic policies has been significantly influenced by a combination of institutional and political constraints. This ideological constraint on social policymaking has resulted in a condensed pattern of population structure and demographic change, a pattern that has progressed at a pace much faster than that

---

[68] On 29 October 2015, the central government introduced and approved the "universal two-child policy" during the Fifth Plenary Session of the 18th CCP Central Committee meeting. The official announcement and endorsement of the universal two-child policy were subsequently made in Chinese Communist Party Central Committee, Document No. 40. 2015. "Zhonggong zhongyang guowuyuan guanyu shishi quanmian lianghai zhengce gaige wanshan jihua shengyu fuwu guanli de jueding (Decision of the Central Committee of the CCP and the State Council on Implementing the Universal Two-Child Policy and Reforming and Improving the Management of Family Planning Services)". Beijing: Chinese Communist Party Central Committee, 31 December 2015.

[69] State Council of People's Republic of China, Document No. 87. 2016. "Guowuyuan guanyu yinfa guojia renkou fazhan guihua 2016–2030 nian de tongzhi (Circular of the State Council on 'Printing and Issuing the National Plan for the Population Development 2016–2030)". Beijing: The State Council of People's Republic of China, 30 December 2016.

[70] See, Chinese Communist Party Central Committee, Document No. 30. 2021. "Zhonggong zhongyang guowuyuan guanyu youhua shengyu zhengce cujin renkou changqi junheng fazhan de jueding (Decision of the Central Committee of the CCP and the State Council on Optimizing Fertility Policies to Promote Long-Term Balanced Development of the Population)". Beijing: Chinese Communist Party Central Committee, 26 June 2021.

observed in other transitional countries with comparable per capita GDP to China.

While China possessed a substantial labour force and a favourable labour structure relative to many other countries during its post-war economic transition, it faced a deficit in essential social policymaking mechanisms. These mechanisms are not only responsive to political exigencies but are also designed to adapt to evolving population structures in expectation of future labour market and economic requirements. In the absence of a well-established and enduring demographic policy institution, China would be confronted with the challenge of a rapid decline in labour supply and a deteriorating population structure before it could effectively ascend to the high-income category.

As a crucial factor input, an abundant labour supply played a substantial role in driving China's economic and income growth throughout the 1990s and 2000s. When the Chinese government began relaxing its birth control policies in 2013, there were high expectations that this would lead to an increase in the country's birth rate, potentially alleviating labour market pressures, at least in the short term. However, by the time the constraints of ideology in central policymaking were eventually lifted in 2013, China had already commenced experiencing declines in both labour force participation and its overall population.

Today's China continues to exhibit relatively favourable labour market conditions in comparison with other East Asian countries, such as Japan and South Korea. However, a pressing concern arises as the nation remains situated within the upper-middle-income group, despite the onset of a decline in its working-age population ratio. Therefore, the deteriorating labour market conditions observed since the mid-2010s appear to signify an intercepting phase, one that has the potential to impede China's future growth momentum.

Upon a comprehensive examination of China's population policy changes and the accelerated demographic trends, it becomes evident that the role of population policies in instigating a rapid demographic transition is paramount. This insight will serve as a foundational premise for the subsequent analysis in the forthcoming chapter, wherein the dual transitions of China's quick economic and income advancements are intricately intertwined with its condensed demographic transition, either propelling or constraining its progress.

# REFERENCES

Attane, Isabelle. 2002. "China's Family Planning Policy: An Overview of Its Past and Future." *Studies in Family Planning* 33(1):103–113.

Becker, Gary S. 1964. *Human Capital: A Theoretical and Empirical Analysis with Special Reference to Education.* New York: Columbia University Press.

Bloom, David E., David Canning, and Günther Fink. 2010. "Implications of Population Ageing for Economic Growth." *Oxford Review of Economic Policy* 26(4): 583–612.

Cai, Fang. 2008. *Liuyisi zhuanzhedian: zhongguo jingji fazhan xin jieduan (Lewis Turning Point: A Coming New Stage of Chinas Economic Development).* Beijing: Social Sciences Academic Press.

Cai, Fang. 2010. "Demographic Transition, Demographic Dividend, and Lewis Turning Point in China." *China Economic Journal* 3(2):107–119.

Chinese Communist Party Central Committee. 1980. "Zhonggong zhongyang guanyu kongzhi woguo renkou zengzhang wenti zhi quanti gongchan dangyuan gongqing tuanyuan de gongkaixi (The Open Letter to all CCP Members and the Chinese Youth League Members about Controls on Our Country's Population Growth)". Beijing: Renmin ribao (*People's Daily*), 25 September 1980.

Chinese Communist Party Central Committee, Document No. 698. 1962. "Zhonggong zhongyang guowuyuan guanyu renzhen tichang jihua shengyu de zhishi (Instruction on Earnestly Advocating Family Planning)." Beijing: Chinese Communist Party Central Committee, 18 December 1962.

Chinese Communist Party Central Committee, Document No. 13. 1986. "Zhonggong zhongyang zhuanfa guojia jishengwei guanyu 'liu wu' qijian jihua shengyu gongzuo qingkuang he 'qi wu' qijian gongzuo yijian de baogao (Circular of the Chinese Communist Party Central Committee on Forwarding 'the Report of National Family Planning Commission on the Work of Family Planning During the Sixth Five-year Plan and on the Opinion of Work During the Seventh Five-year Plan')." Beijing: Chinese Communist Party Central Committee, 9 May 1986.

Chinese Communist Party Central Committee, Document No. 9. 1991. "Zhonggong zhongyang guowuyuan guanyu jiaqiang jihua shengyu gongzuo yange kongzhi renkou zengzhang de jueding (Decision of the CCP Central Committee and the State Council on Strengthening the Work of Family Planning and Strictly Controlling Population Growth)." Beijing: Chinese Communist Party Central Committee, 12 May 1991.

Chinese Communist Party Central Committee, Document No. 8. 2000. "Zhonggong zhongyang guowuyuan guanyu jiaqiang renkou yu jihua shengyu gongzuo wending di shengyu shuiping de jueding (Decision of the CCP Central Committee and the State Council on 'Strengthening the Work

of Population and Family Planning and Stabilising Low Fertility Level')."
Beijing: Chinese Communist Party Central Committee, 2 March 2000.

Chinese Communist Party Central Committee, Document No. 22. 2006.
"Zhonggong zhongyang guowuyuan yinfa guanyu quanmian jiaqiang renkou
he jihua shengyu gongzuo tongchou jiejue renkou wenti de jueding (Deci-
sion of the Central Committee of the CCP Central Committee and the
State Council on 'Comprehensively Strengthening of Population and Family
Planning Work and Solving the Population Problem')." Beijing: Chinese
Communist Party Central Committee, 17 December 2006.

Chinese Communist Party Central Committee, Document No. 12. 2013.
"Zhonggong zhongyang guanyu quanmian shenhua gaige ruogan zhongda
wenti de jueding (Decision of the CCP Central Committee on Some
Major Issues Concerning Comprehensively Deepening the Reform)." Beijing:
The Third Session of the Eighteenth Central Committee of the Chinese
Communist Party, 12 November 2013.

Chinese Communist Party Central Committee, Document No. 15. 2013.
"Zhonggong zhongyang guowuyuan yinfa guanyu tiaozheng wanshan
shengyu zhengce de yijian (Opinions Issued by the CCP Central Committee
and the State Council on 'Adjusting and Improving the Family Planning
Policy')." Beijing: 30 December 2013.

Chinese Communist Party Central Committee, Document No. 40. 2015.
"Zhonggong zhongyang guowuyuan guanyu shishi quanmian lianghai
zhengce gaige wanshan jihua shengyu fuwu guanli de jueding (Decision of the
Central Committee of the CCP and the State Council on Implementing the
Universal Two-Child Policy and Reforming and Improving the Management
of Family Planning Services)." Beijing: Chinese Communist Party Central
Committee, 31 December 2015.

Chinese Communist Party Central Committee, Document No. 30. 2021.
"Zhonggong zhongyang guowuyuan guanyu youhua shengyu zhengce cujin
renkou changqi junheng fazhan de jueding (Decision of the Central
Committee of the CCP and the State Council on Optimizing Fertility Policies
to Promote Long-Term Balanced Development of the Population)." Beijing:
Chinese Communist Party Central Committee, 26 June 2021.

Chinese Communist Party Central Committee and the Ministry of Health,
Document No. 45. 1955. "Zhonggong zhongyang dui weisheng bu dangzu
guanyu jiezhi shengyu wenti de baogao de pishi (Instructions of the CCP
Central Committee on the report of the Ministry of Health' Party Committee
on the Issues of Birth Control)." Beijing: Chinese Communist Party Central
Committee and the Ministry of Health, 1 March 1955.

DiMaio, Alfred J. 1980. "The Soviet Union and Population: Theory, Problems,
and Population Policy." *Comparative Political Studies* 13(1):97–136.

Heoffding, Oleg. 1963. "Sino-Soviet Economic Relations, 1959–1962." *Communist China and the Soviet Bloc* 349:94–105.

Hesketh, Therese, Lu Li, and Wei Xing Zhu. 2005. "The Effect of China's One-Child Family Policy after 25 Years." *New England Journal of Medicine* 353(11):1171–1176.

Information Office of the State Council of PRC. 2000. "Zhongguo 21 shiji renkou yu fazhan (China's Population and Development in the 21st Century)." *White Paper of the Government of PRC.* Beijing: Information Office of the State Council of the People's Republic of China, December 2000.

Jin, Cheng. 2017. *An Economic Analysis of the Rise and Decline of Chinese Township and Village Enterprises.* Basingstoke: Palgrave Macmillan.

Lewis, William Arthur. 1972. "Reflections on Unlimited Labour." In Di Marco, Luis Eugenio (ed.). *International Economics and Development: Essays in Hornor of Raul Prebisch.* New York: Elsevier, pp. 75–96.

Li, Daokiu, and Xiang Xu. 2012. *Zhongguo renkou yu laodong wenti baogao No.13: renkou zhuanbian yu zhongguo jingji zai pingheng (Reports on China's Population and Labour No. 13: Demographic Transition and Economic Rebalance in China).* Beijing: Social Sciences Academic Press.

Liang, Jianzhang, and Jianxin Li. 2012. *Zhongguo ren taiduo le ma? (Too Many People in China?).* Beijing: Social Sciences Academic Press.

Lin, Justin Yifu. 2013. *Shengyu zhengce tiaozheng yu zhongguo fazhan (Fertility Policy Adjustment and Development in China).* Beijing: Social Sciences Academic Press.

Literature Research Office of the Central Committee of Chinese Communist Party. 1982. *San zhong quanhui yilai zhongyao wenxian xuanbian (Selected Important Documents Since the Third Plenary Session of the 11th Central Committee of Chinese Communist Party).* Beijing: People's Publishing House.

Liu, Haoming. 2014. "The Quality–quantity Trade-off: Evidence from the Relaxation of China's One-Child Policy." *Journal of Population Economics* 27(2):565–602.

Lu, Feng. 2011. "Zhongguo nongaming gong gongzi dingliang guce 1979–2010 (Quantitative Estimation of Wage Rates for Chinese Migrant Workers 1979–2010)." *China Centre for Economic Research Working Paper Series* No. C2011020. Published on 18 November 2011. Available at https://nsd.pku.edu.cn/pub/chnsd/attachments/6548c6f9e6314a4fb20a4efdec5ff4a2.pdf, accessed 15 August 2023.

Ma, Yinchu. 1957. "Xin renkou lun(The New Population Theory)." *Renmin ribao (People's Daily)*, published on 5 July 1957.

Mao, Zedong. 1951 [1991]. "Weixin lishi guang de pochan (The Bankruptcy of Idealist Historiography)." In Mao, Zedong. *Mao Zedong xuanji (Selected*

*Works of Mao Tse-Tung*) 4:1511–1512. Beijing: Renmin chuban she (People's Publishing House).

McElroy, Marjorie, and Dennis Tao Yang. 2000. "Carrots and Sticks: Fertility Effects of China's Population Policies." *The American Economic Review* 90(2):389–392.

National Bureau of Statistics. 2009. Xin Zhongguo chengli 60 zhounian xilie baogao zhiwu: renkou zongliang shidu zengzhang jiegou mingxian gaishan (New China 60th Anniversary Report Series No. 5: Moderate Increase in Total Population and Significant Improvement in Its Structure). Available at https://www.gov.cn/test/2009-09/15/content_1417725.htm, accessed 15 August 2023.

National Bureau of Statistics of China. 2013. *Migrant Workers Monitoring Survey Report 2012.* Available at https://www.gov.cn/gzdt/2013-05/27/content_2411923.htm, accessed 15 August 2023.

National Bureau of Statistics of China. 2018. *Migrant Workers Monitoring Survey Report 2017.* Available at https://app.www.gov.cn/govdata/gov/201804/28/423387/article.html, accessed 15 August 2023.

National Bureau of Statistics of China. 2023. *Migrant Workers Monitoring Survey Report 2022.* Available at http://www.stats.gov.cn/sj/zxfb/202304/t20230427_1939124.html, accessed 15 August 2023.

National Bureau of Statistics of China. (n.d.). National Data. Available at https://data.stats.gov.cn/english/easyquery.htm?cn=C01, accessed 15 August 2023.

National Bureau of Statistics of China. (n.d.). *Zhongguo Tongji Nianjian (China Statistical Yearbook).* Beijing: China Statistics Press.

National People's Congress. 2001. *Population and Family Planning Law of the People's Republic of China 2002.* Beijing: The Twenty-fifth Session of Standing Committee of the Ninth National People's Congress and Promulgated for Implementation by the Proclamation of the National People's Congress, 29 December 2001.

National People's Congress of People Republic of China. 1978. *Constitution of the People's Republic of China 1978.* Beijing: The First Session of the Fifth National People's Congress and Promulgated for Implementation by the Proclamation of the National People's Congress, 5 April 1978.

National People's Congress of People Republic of China. 1980. *Marriage Law of The People's Republic of China 1981.* Beijing: The Third Session of the Fifth National People's Congress and Promulgated for Implementation by the Proclamation of the National People's Congress, 10 September 1980.

National People's Congress of People Republic of China. 1982. *Constitution of the People's Republic of China 1982.* Beijing: The Fifth Session of the Fifth National People's Congress and Promulgated for Implementation by the Proclamation of the National People's Congress, 4 December 1978.

OECD. (n.d.). Historical Population Data and Projections (1950–2050). Available at https://stats.oecd.org/index.aspx?DataSetCode=POP_PROJ, accessed 15 August 2023.

Peng, Peiyun. 1997. *Zhongguo jihua shengyu quanshu* (*A Complete Book on Chinese Family Planning*). Beijing: China Population Publishing House.

Peng, Xizhe. 2011. "China's Demographic History and Future Challenges." *Science* 333(6042):581–587.

Polaris, Jean. 1964. "The Sino-Soviet Dispute: Its Impact on China." *International Affairs* 40(4):647–658.

Ruoshui. 1959. "Renkou yu renshou (Population and Manpower)." *Renmin ribao* (*People's Daily*), 15 April 1959.

Scharping, Thomas. 2003. *Birth Control in China 1949–2000: Population Policy and Demographic Development*. London: Routledge.

Schultz, Theodore W. 1963. *Economic Value of Education*. New York: Columbia University Press.

Schultz, T. Paul, and Yi Zeng. 1995. "Fertility of Rural China. Effects of Local Family Planning and Health Programs". *Journal of Population Economics* 8(4):329–350.

State Council of People Republic of China. Document No. 51. 1971. "Guowuyuan zhuanfa weishengbu junguanhui shangyebu ranliao huaxue gongyebu guanyu zuohao jihua shengyu gongzuo de baogao (Circular of the State Council on Forwarding on the Military Control Commission of Ministry of Health, the Ministry of Commerce and the Ministry of Chemical Industry's 'Report on Better Implementing Family Planning Policy')." Beijing: The State Council of People Republic of China, 8 July 1971.

State Council of People's Republic of China, Document No. 39. 2011. "Guowuyuan guanyu yinfa guojia renkou fazhan 'shi er wu' guihua de tongzhi (Circular of the State Council on Printing and Issuing 'the National "12th Five-Year Plan" for Population Development')." Beijing: The State Council of People's Republic of China, 23 November 2011.

State Council of People's Republic of China, Document No. 87. 2016. "Guowuyuan guanyu yinfa guojia renkou fazhan guihua 2016–2030 nian de tongzhi (Circular of the State Council on 'Printing and Issuing the National Plan for the Population Development 2016–2030)." Beijing: The State Council of People's Republic of China, 30 December 2016.

The Conference Board. 2016. International Comparisons of Hourly Compensation Costs in Manufacturing and Sub-Manufacturing Industries. Available at https://www.conference-board.org/retrievefile.cfm?filename=ilccompensationtimeseries_2016.xlsx, accessed 15 August 2023.

The World Bank. (n.d.). World Development Indicators. Washington: The World Bank. Available at https://datacatalog.worldbank.org/dataset/world-development-indicators, accessed 15 August 2023.

United Nations. 2001. *World Population Ageing, 1950–2050*. https://www.un.org/development/desa/pd/sites/www.un.org.development.desa.pd/files/files/documents/2021/Nov/undesa_pd_2002_wpa_1950-2050_web.pdf, accessed 15 August 2023.

United Nations, Department of Economic and Social Affairs, Population Division. 2022. *World Population Prospects 2022*. Available at https://population.un.org/wpp/, accessed 15 August 2023.

Wang, Cuntong. 2012. "History of the Chinese Family Planning Program: 1970–2010." *Contraception* 85(6):563–569.

Wang, Feng, and Andrew Mason. 2008. "The Demographic Factor in China's Transition." In Brandt, Loren, and Thomas G. Rawski (eds.). *China's Great Economic Transformation*. Cambridge: Cambridge University Press, pp. 136–166.

Wang, Fei, Liqiu Zhao, and Zhong Zhao. 2017. "China's Family Planning Policies and Their Labor Market Consequences." *Journal of Population Economics* 30(1):31–68.

Weil, David N. 1997. "The Economics of Population Aging." *Handbook of Population and Family Economics* 1(B):967–1014.

Whyte, Martin King, Wang Feng, and Yong Cai. 2015. "Challenging Myths about China's One-Child Policy". *The China Journal* 74:144–159.

Yao, Yang. 2011. "The Relationship between China's Export-led Growth and Its Double Transition of Demographic Change and Industrialization." *Asian Economic Papers* 10(2):52–76.

Zhang, Junsen. 2017. "The Evolution of China's One-Child Policy and Its Effects on Family Outcomes". *Journal of Economic Perspectives* 31(1):141–160.

CHAPTER 3

# China's Dual Transition: Income Growth and Transitioning Demographics

**Abstract** This chapter undertakes a comparative examination of post-war economic development and income transitions in China, as well as selected East and Southeast Asian economies. In parallel with China, both Japan and South Korea have witnessed a transformation from high post-war birth and fertility rates to low ones, culminating in overall population declines. However, a noteworthy distinction emerges when considering that Japan and South Korea transitioned into upper middle-income economies and subsequently achieved high-income status while maintaining population structures characterized by a predominant presence of young and middle-aged working individuals. China, conversely, represents a contrasting scenario in this regard.

**Keywords** Income transition · Demographic transition · Post-war economic transition · Asian Tigers · Asian miracle · Demographic structure · Lewis turning point · Demographic dividend · Population window period · Japan · South Korea · Taiwan

© The Author(s), under exclusive license to Springer Nature Switzerland AG 2024
J. Du, *China's Labour Market, 1950–2050*, Palgrave Studies in Economic History, https://doi.org/10.1007/978-3-031-53138-5_3

## Dynamics of China's Income Transition

China has benefited greatly from its demographic dividend, with a substantial working-age population contributing to economic growth through increased domestic consumer demand, large savings and investments, and heightened productivity. The country has achieved remarkable economic growth, progressing to the status of a newly industrialized country within East Asia. In 2009, China successfully ascended to the classification of an upper-middle-income economy, as per the World Bank's categorization (see Table 3.1). By 2022, China's per capita GDP had risen to US$12,720.2 at current prices.[1]

The fast economic growth in China has led to a significant enhancement of living standards among its populace. Social development initiatives have brought about considerable improvements in demographic indicators, including increased life expectancy, enhanced adult literacy rates, and reduced infant mortality rates among the Chinese population. Despite the rapid transition and commendable social development achievements, pivotal questions persist regarding China's ability to attain the status of a high-income nation and, perhaps even more importantly, how sustainable this status will be in the face of the country's quickly evolving demographic trends.

Cross-country analysis reveals that attaining high-income status for developing economies has become increasingly challenging in recent decades. According to the World Bank's classifications, since 1990, only a few Asian nations have successfully achieved high-income status. These include[2] Oman (in 2007), Macau (in 1994), and the two Asian Tigers, Taiwan (in 1993), and South Korea (in 1995/2001).[3] When considering industrialization as the primary factor, only Taiwan and South Korea have solidly transitioned past the middle-income classification, supported by

---

[1] The World Bank. (n.d.). *World Development Indicators*. Washington: The World Bank. Available at https://datacatalog.worldbank.org/dataset/world-development-indicators, accessed 15 August 2023.

[2] Former high-income economies that downgraded to middle-income status but subsequently regained high-income status after 1990 were excluded.

[3] South Koreas firstly ascended to the high-income group in 1995, but experienced a subsequent downgrade to upper-middle-income status during the 1997 Asian Financial Crisis. It was not until 2001 that the country ultimately regained high-income status, solidifying its position among the Four Asian Tigers, which include Japan, Hong Kong, and Singapore.

**Table 3.1**  World Bank's analytical classifications of income based on per capita gross national income (GNI) in US dollars

| Year (1) | Low income (2) | Lower-middle-income (3) | Upper-middle-income (4) | High-income (5) |
|---|---|---|---|---|
| 1987 | ≤480 | 481–1,940 | 1,941–6,000 | >6,000 |
| 1988 | ≤545 | 546–2,200 | 2,201–6,000 | >6,000 |
| 1989 | ≤580 | 581–2,335 | 2,336–6,000 | >6,000 |
| 1990 | ≤610 | 611–2,465 | 2,466–7,620 | >7,620 |
| 1991 | ≤635 | 636–2,555 | 2,556–7,910 | >7,910 |
| 1992 | ≤675 | 676–2,695 | 2,696–8,355 | >8,355 |
| 1993 | ≤695 | 696–2,785 | 2,786–8,625 | >8,625 |
| 1994 | ≤725 | 726–2,895 | 2,896–8,955 | >8,955 |
| 1995 | ≤765 | 766–3,035 | 3,036–9,385 | >9,385 |
| 1996 | ≤785 | 786–3,115 | 3,116–9,645 | >9,645 |
| 1997 | ≤785 | 786–3,125 | 3,126–9,655 | >9,655 |
| 1998 | ≤760 | 761–3,030 | 3,031–9,360 | >9,360 |
| 1999 | ≤755 | 756–2,995 | 2,996–9,265 | >9,265 |
| 2000 | ≤755 | 756–2,995 | 2,996–9,265 | >9,265 |
| 2001 | ≤745 | 746–2,975 | 2,976–9,205 | >9,205 |
| 2002 | ≤735 | 736–2,935 | 2,936–9,075 | >9,075 |
| 2003 | ≤765 | 766–3,035 | 3,036–9,385 | >9,385 |
| 2004 | ≤825 | 826–3,255 | 3,256–10,065 | >10,065 |
| 2005 | ≤875 | 876–3,465 | 3,466–10,725 | >10,725 |
| 2006 | ≤905 | 906–3,595 | 3,596–11,115 | >11,115 |
| 2007 | ≤935 | 936–3,705 | 3,706–11,455 | >11,455 |
| 2008 | ≤975 | 976–3,855 | 3,856–11,905 | >11,905 |
| 2009 | ≤995 | 996–3,945 | 3,946–12,195 | >12,195 |
| 2010 | ≤1,005 | 1,006–3,975 | 3,976–12,275 | >12,275 |
| 2011 | ≤1,025 | 1,026–4,035 | 4,036–12,475 | >12,475 |
| 2012 | ≤1,035 | 1,036–4,085 | 4,086–12,615 | >12,615 |
| 2013 | ≤1,045 | 1,046–4,125 | 4,126–12,745 | >12,745 |
| 2014 | ≤1,045 | 1,046–4,125 | 4,126–12,735 | >12,735 |
| 2015 | ≤1,025 | 1,026–4,035 | 4,036–12,475 | >12,475 |
| 2016 | ≤1,005 | 1,006–3,955 | 3,956–12,235 | >12,235 |
| 2017 | ≤995 | 996–3,895 | 3,896–12,055 | >12,055 |
| 2018 | ≤1,025 | 1,026–3,995 | 3,996–12,375 | >12,375 |
| 2019 | ≤1,035 | 1,036–4,045 | 4,046–12,535 | >12,535 |
| 2020 | ≤1,045 | 1,046–4,095 | 4,096–12,695 | >12,695 |
| 2021 | ≤1,085 | 1,086–4,255 | 4,256–13,205 | >13,205 |

*Source* World Bank. 2022. *World Bank GNI Per Capita Operational Guidelines and Analytical Classifications.* Available at http://databank.worldbank.org/data/download/site-content/OGH IST.xls, accessed 15 August 2023

robust economic fundamentals. In contrast, Oman's growth has been driven by its energy sector, while Macau's economy relies heavily on tourism. Therefore, transitioning out of the middle-income group poses a significant challenge, akin to a potential "trap", for many developing Asian economies in the present context.

The term "middle-income trap" refers to a situation in which economies attain middle-income status but then experience a deceleration in their growth, causing them to remain in the middle-income bracket for an extended period. The widely accepted classification system developed by the World Bank categorizes economies based on their GNI per capita, as illustrated in Table 3.1[4] and tracks these classifications over time in conjunction with global economic growth trends. The overarching objective of income transition is to elevate the living standard to a level comparable to that of the most developed economies today. Therefore, defining thresholds based on relative growth rates concerning high-income economies may provide a more comprehensive framework for capturing the dynamics of China's income transition.

The approach of comparing GDP per capita relative to that of the United States has been widely adopted to analyse the dynamics of income transition.[5] Following the methodology employed in a World Bank report,[6] namely 10% and 50%, have been selected to delineate middle- and high-income categories, respectively. Figure 3.1 illustrates the long-term income transition dynamics of various economies over the period from 1960 to 2022.[7] Economies positioned in the top-left and top-middle quadrants are those that have successfully moved out of the

---

[4] For details, see the World Bank. (n.d.). *World Bank Atlas Method—Detailed Methodology*. Available at datahelpdesk.worldbank.org/knowledgebase/articles/378832-what-is-the-world-bank-atlas-method, accessed 15 August 2023.

[5] See, Im, Fernando Gabriel, and David Rosenblatt. 2013. "Middle-Income Traps: A Conceptual and Empirical Survey." *Policy Research Working Paper* No. WPS 6594. Washington, DC: World Bank.

[6] This analysis adheres to the methodology presented by Bulman, Eden and Nguyen (2014), employing the middle-income and high-income thresholds of 10% and 50%, respectively. For more information, please refer to Bulman, David, Maya Eden, and Ha Nguyen. 2017. "Transitioning from Low-Income Growth to High-Income Growth: Is There a Middle-Income Trap?" *Policy Research Working Paper* No. WPS 646. Washington, DC: World Bank.

[7] Due to data limitations, Fig. 3.1 exclusively plots countries with available data from 1960 to 2022.

middle-income category, while those in the left-middle quadrant have made the transition from low-income status.

Figure 3.1 shows a high degree of persistence in the relative economic status of most economies. Many of the high-income economies in 1960 maintained their high-income status through to 2022. Several middle-income economies have successfully transitioned to high-income status, but a significant majority have remained within the middle-income group. Over the past six decades, a large number of economies have remained classified as low-income, with only a few managing to advance to the middle-income category.

In the Asian context, Japan has steadily progressed to become a consistently high-income economy, while Singapore achieved rapid economic growth, elevating its per capita GDP even higher than that of the United

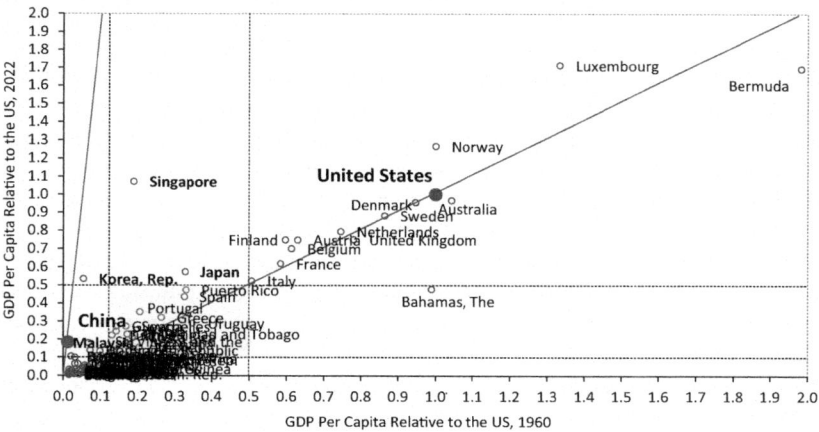

**Fig. 3.1** GDP per capita relative to the US (constant 2015 US$), 1960 vs. 2022 (*Source* The World Bank. [n.d.]. *World Development Indicators*. Washington: The World Bank. Available at https://datacatalog.worldbank.org/dat aset/world-development-indicators, accessed 15 August 2023)

States. South Korea has made strides and now stands on the cusp of high-income status.[8] Malaysia has slipped towards middle-income trap, while China has transitioned from a low-income to a middle-income economy.

Based on the data analysis for the year 2022, particularly as depicted in Fig. 3.1, it is evident that China continues to follow the fastest trajectory in its income transition. In other words, given the prevailing conditions, China remains less susceptible to succumbing to the middle-income trap. Nevertheless, the central question revolves around China's prospects for further income transition, considering the concurrent rapid evolution of its demographic trends, rather than whether China is irrevocably ensnared in the middle-income category.

## INCOME TRANSITIONS IN SELECTED ASIAN ECONOMIES

### Post-war Income Transition in East and Southeast Asia

China's income transition over the past four decades becomes more comprehensible when examined within the broader context of middle-income transitions in East and Southeast Asia. In the post-war period, many developing economies in this region collectively demonstrated a faster trajectory of growth in comparison with the rest of the world. Several East and Southeast Asian economies initiated their economic take-off during the 1950s and 1960s, exemplified by economies such as Hong Kong, Singapore, and Taiwan. A few economies, which lately broke away from the Cold War[9] ideology associated with the Soviet Union, embarked on their transition during the 1970s and 1980s, as seen in the cases of China and Vietnam.

Empirically, as presented in Table 3.2, from the list of 15 economies in the East and Southeast Asia (excluding Macao and Brunei), Japan, Hong Kong, Singapore, Taiwan, and South Korea have achieved a

---

[8] Taiwan is not listed in this figure due to its exclusion from the *World Development Indicator* database.

[9] The Cold War was a period of intense geopolitical tension that emerged between the Soviet Union and the United States, along with their respective allies, following the conclusion of WWII. Although there was no direct large-scale armed conflict between the two superpowers, they provided support to opposing factions in significant global conflicts. These actions were driven by an ideological and geopolitical competition for global influence. The Cold War came to an end with the collapse of the Soviet Union in 1991.

successful transition to high-income status from middle-income classification. Malaysia, Thailand, and China have advanced to upper-middle-income group. In contrast, the Philippines, Indonesia, Vietnam, Myanmar, Cambodia, Mongolia, and Laos have made the transition from the low-income category to the lower-middle-income category.

East and Southeast Asian economies can be categorized into three tiers based their economic ranking, as indicated by per capita GDP:

- Economies that are progressing towards persistent high-income status, with GDP per capita consistently at approximately US$40,000 and above. Examples include Japan, Hong Kong, and Singapore.
- Recently developed economies with GDP per capita ranging between US$30,000 and US$40,000, such as Taiwan and South Korea.
- The remaining 12 economies, which upgraded to middle-income status during the 1990s–2000s with per capita GDP of US$13,000 or less. This group includes China, Malaysia, Thailand, Mongolia, Indonesia, Vietnam, the Philippines, and others.

An examination of transitions in Fig. 3.2, comparing recent developments with earlier periods, reveals that the grouping of economies based on GDP per capita rankings has remained largely consistent throughout the period from 1960 to 2021. The only notable change is the degradation of the Philippines from the second tier to the bottom of the third tier.[10]

While the rankings have remained relatively consistent, the pathways of transition have exhibited significant variations. Figure 3.3 depicts the relationship between the year an economy entered the lower-middle-income category and the duration it remained in that tier before advancing to the upper-middle-income group. This analysis utilizes the data presented in Table 3.2 and aims to provide insights into the dynamics of income transition in Asia. This is to understand the dynamics of Asia's income transition, against the backdrop of which China is experiencing in its ongoing transition to high-income.

---

[10] The economic growth of Brunei Darussalam has predominantly been propelled by its energy sector.

**Table 3.2** Income transition in selected East and Southeast Asian economies

| | | High-income economies in 2022 | | | | |
| --- | --- | --- | --- | --- | --- | --- |
| | | Year turned lower-middle-income (1) | Year turned upper-middle-income (2) | Year turned high-income (3) | Years in lower-middle-income (4) | Years in upper-middle-income (5) |
| East Asia | Japan | 1933 | 1968 | 1977 | 36 | 10 |
| East Asia | Hong Kong | 1950 | 1976 | 1983 | 27 | 8 |
| Southeast Asia | Singapore | 1950 | 1978 | 1988 | 30 | 11 |
| East Asia | Taiwan | 1967 | 1986 | 1993 | 20 | 8 |
| East Asia | Korea, S. | 1969 | 1988 | 1995 | 20 | 8 |

| | | Upper-middle-income economies in 2022 | | | |
| --- | --- | --- | --- | --- | --- |
| | | Year turned lower-middle-income (6) | Year turned upper-middle-income (7) | Years in lower-middle-income (8) | Years in upper-middle-income by 2022 (9) |
| Southeast Asia | Malaysia | 1969 | 1996 | 28 | 27 |
| Southeast Asia | Thailand | 1976 | 2004 | 29 | 19 |
| East Asia | China | 1992 | 2009 | 18 | 14 |

*Lower-middle-income economies in 2022*

| | | Year turned lower-middle-income (10) | Years in lower-middle-income by 2022 (11) |
|---|---|---|---|
| Southeast Asia | Philippines | 1975 | 48 |
| Southeast Asia | Indonesia | 1986 | 37 |
| Southeast Asia | Vietnam | 2002 | 21 |
| Southeast Asia | Myanmar | 2004 | 19 |
| Southeast Asia | Cambodia | 2006 | 17 |
| East Asia | Mongolia | 2007 | 18 |
| Southeast Asia | Laos | 2012 | 11 |

*Source* Compiled by the author using data collected from Felipe, Jesus, Utsav Kumar, and Reynold Galope. 2014. "Middle-Income Transitions: Trap or Myth?" *Asian Development Bank Economics Working Paper Series* No. 421. Available at www.adb.org/sites/default/files/publication/149903/ewp-421.pdf, accessed 15 August 2023

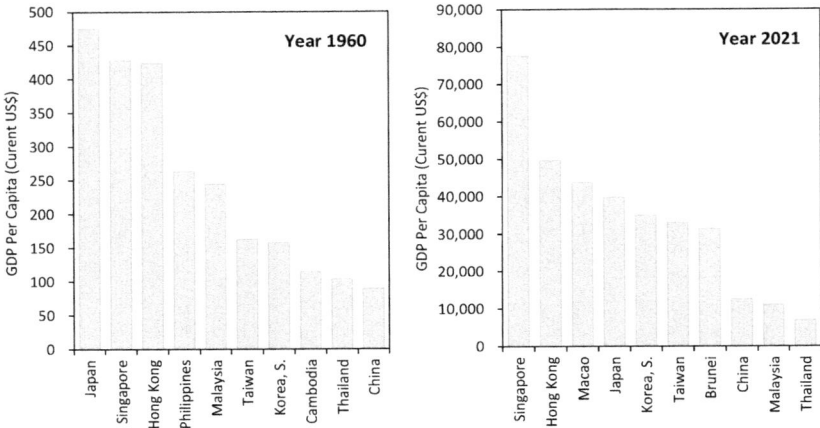

**Fig. 3.2** GDP per capita for selected East and Southeast Asian economies, 1960 vs. 2021 (*Source* The World Bank. [n.d.]. *World Development Indicators*. Washington: The World Bank. Available at https://datacatalog.worldbank.org/dataset/world-development-indicators, accessed 15 August 2023; Directorate-General of Budget, Accounting and Statistics of Taiwan. 2022. *Statistical Yearbook of Taiwan 2022*. Available at https://eng.stat.gov.tw/cl.aspx?n=2574, accessed 15 August 2023)

The average duration spent by the developed economies of East and Southeast Asia, in Table 3.2, for the transition to upper-middle-income status is 26.4 years. Meanwhile, the average for newly industrialized economies, including Malaysia, Thailand, and China, stands at 25 years. These findings suggest that contemporary economic transitions from lower- to upper-middle-income status in Asia have taken approximately the same number of years as historical transitions in the region.

In comparison with the first-tier economies (Japan, Hong Kong, and Singapore), Taiwan and South Korea in the second tier achieved the transition from lower- to upper-middle-income status in just 20 years, as illustrated in panel *a* of Fig. 3.3. This expedited progress can be largely attributed to the valuable lessons gleaned from the income transition experiences of their first-tier predecessors, which accelerated their own process. By the end of 2022, Malaysia (28 years) and Thailand (29 years) in the third tier had experienced slower transitions to upper-middle-income during the late 1990s and early 2000s. In contrast, China

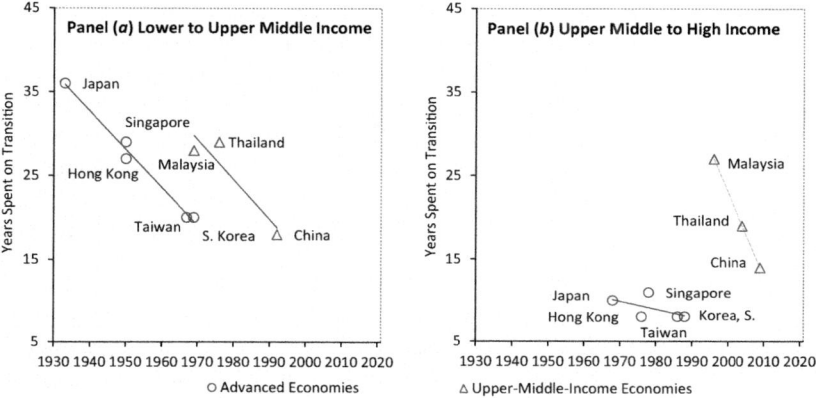

**Fig. 3.3** Upper-middle-income and high-income transitions in selected East and Southeast Asian economies by 2022 (*Source* Compiled by the author based on information listed in Table 3.2. Felipe, Jesus, Utsav Kumar, and Reynold Galope. 2014. "Middle-Income Transitions: Trap or Myth?" *Asian Development Bank Economics Working Paper Series* No. 421. Available at www.adb.org/sites/default/files/publication/149903/ewp-421.pdf, accessed 15 August 2023)

accomplished the fastest transition, completing the change from lower- to upper-middle-income status in just 19 years, spanning the period from 1992 to 2009.[11] Notably, Indonesia and the Philippines have yet to attain upper-middle-income status, despite spending 37 and 48 years in the lower-middle-income group respectively.

In East and Southeast Asia, five economies successfully transitioned from upper-middle-income to high-income status during the period spanning the 1970s to the 1990s, primarily driven by the process of Asian industrialization. These economies include Japan, Hong Kong, Singapore, Taiwan, and South Korea. On average, economies that were already in the upper-middle-income category required a shorter timeframe to progress to the next income level than those transitioning from lower- to upper-middle-income.

---

[11] Mongolia can be considered, to some extent, a resource-based economy with dependent on its coal industry. Given that Mongolia's transition path did not follow a trajectory of non-resource-based industrialization, it has been excluded from the analysis presented here.

At present, advanced economies in East and Southeast Asia, on average, require nine years to progress from the upper-middle to the high-income category. Nonetheless, there has been a noticeable deceleration in the speed of this transition. As illustrated in panel *b* of Fig. 3.3, by 2022, Thailand and China had remained in the upper-middle-income category for 19 and 14 years, respectively. Similarly, Malaysia had sustained its position in the upper-middle-income category for 28 years by 2022, indicating a notably sluggish progression towards achieving high-income status.

Applying the same methodology of comparing relative income transition to that of the United States, the income transitions of East and Southeast Asian economies over the past century can be characterized as a catch-up process, with Japan serving as the benchmark within the Asian context. Hong Kong and Singapore, in the early 2000s, managed to surpass Japan in terms of per capita GDP, emerging as the most successful followers in this pursuit. In addition to benefiting from the diffusion of industrial technology from Japan, the rapid transition of Hong Kong and Singapore was also facilitated by advantageous geographical locations and external factors, including trade and exchange rate policies. However, in terms of overall economic impact, the income transitions of Hong Kong and Singapore are not as significant as those observed in some medium and large-sized economies within the region, such as Taiwan, South Korea, and China.

Asia also encompasses countries with slower income transitions, such Malaysia, Thailand, Indonesia, and even cases of unsuccessful transitions in the Philippines. Figure 3.3 highlights two critical threshold periods in the income transitions within East and Southeast Asia. In the late 1960s, a discernible breakpoint emerged in the upper-middle-income transition (panel *a* of Fig. 3.3). Following the mid-1990s, the transition from upper-middle to high-income has taken a considerably longer duration (panel *b* of Fig. 3.3).

Generally, the post-war income transitions in East and Southeast Asia exhibit two prominent features:

- The first is a shorter transition period compared to the global average. According to a report by the Asian Development Bank,[12]

[12] Felipe, Jesus, Utsav Kumar, and Reynold Galope. 2014. "Middle Income Transitions: Trap or Myth?" *Asian Development Bank Economics Working Paper Series* No. 421.

which analysed 30 economies that completed the entire transition from lower-middle to high-income, the median duration for this transition globally was 83 years. In contrast, East and Southeast Asian countries accomplished this transition in just three decades, significantly shorter than the global median.

- The second is an uneven pace of transition. On average, economies that initiated their transition after the late 1960s required a considerably longer period to progress from lower- to upper-middle-income status compared to those that commenced earlier. Regarding the transition from upper-middle to high-income status, the mid-1990s marked a significant threshold. Economies that commenced their high-income transition prior to this threshold managed to complete it within a decade. Conversely, those that began after this point have yet to achieve the same level of success as of today.

### *Turning Points in East and Southeast Asia's Income Transitions*

When upgraded to high-income, from the 1960s, Japan began to transfer low-end industries to Asian developing economies. This move sparked labour-intensive industrialization in economically less advanced regions of Asia. Consequently, the rapid income transitions in East and Southeast Asian economies can largely be interpreted as part of a catch-up process, characterized by the continuous adoption of new industrial technologies from Japan.

Factors hindering technological diffusion can exert a restraining influence on income transition, particularly when an economy reaches a stage where these factors significantly disrupt the catch-up process. At crucial junctures, these impediments have the potential to instigate substantial economic divergence. In essence, even a minor alteration in an economy's approach to openness can set it on a distinct transition trajectory from that of its counterparts in rapidly industrializing Asia. To elucidate the distinctive factors contributing to divergence in income transition across Asia, Fig. 3.4 illustrates the transition momentum of selected economies at intervals of 20 years since the 1960s.

Available at www.adb.org/sites/default/files/publication/149903/ewp-421.pdf, accessed 15 August 2023.

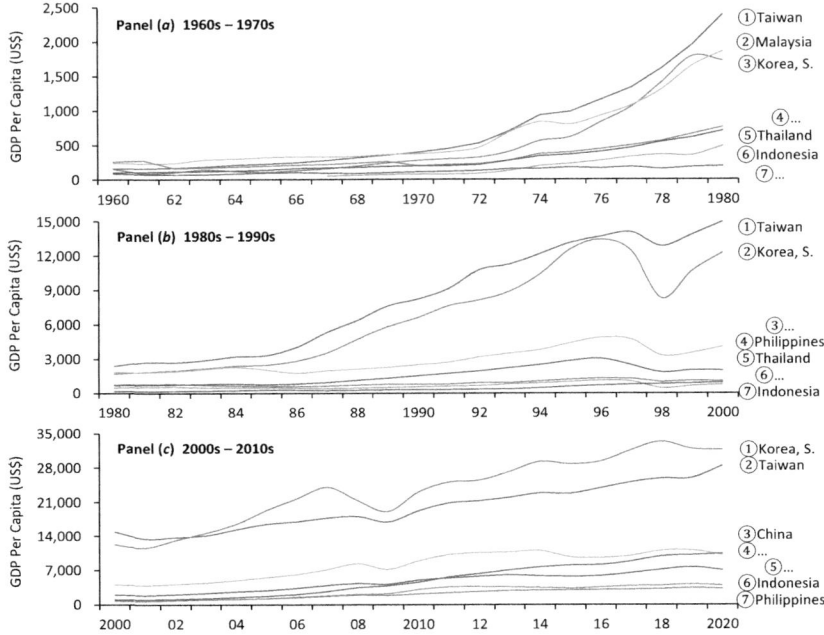

**Fig. 3.4** GDP per capita in selected Asian economies (Current US$), 1960s–2020s (*Source* The World Bank. [n.d.]. *World Development Indicators.* Washington: The World Bank. Available at https://datacatalog.worldbank.org/dataset/world-development-indicators, accessed 15 August 2023; Directorate-General of Budget, Accounting and Statistics of Taiwan. 2022. *Statistical Yearbook of Taiwan 2022.* Available at https://eng.stat.gov.tw/cl.aspx?n=2574, accessed 15 August 2023)

- **The first divergence** of Asia's income transition happened in the 1960s, a period marked by the broader economic emergence of the Asian region. This divergence was primarily influenced by two key factors: the geopolitical tensions of the Cold War and the resurgence of post-war nationalism in Asia.

   After WWII, the political ideologies of numerous East and Southeast Asian economies became increasingly intertwined with the dynamics of the Cold War. The Soviet Union extended its ideological influence into East Asia, as evident in countries like China and

North Korea. Additionally, a set of Warsaw Pact[13] observer countries in Southeast Asia, such as Vietnam, Laos, and Cambodia, had themselves aligned with the Soviet, further solidifying their connection to the communist centrally planned system. This ideological alignment hindered certain Asian economies from accessing industrial technology transfers from Western technology frontiers, resulting in prolonged stays in the low-income classification. For instance, China remained in the low-income group for 43 years before advancing to the lower-middle-income category in 1992. Similarly, Vietnam and Cambodia remained in the low-income category until the 2000s.

Alongside the Cold War-affected countries, the Philippines and Malaysia also pursued a semi-closed economic model, influenced by the rising tide of nationalism. In the case of the Philippines, the anti-Chinese policy known as "Filipino First"[14] had a significant impact on the country's rice economy during the 1960s. This policy was due to the fact that Chinese Filipinos controlled approximately 70% of the country's rice trade and 75% of its rice mills during the war.[15] After a short period of deregulation in the mid-1960s, the Philippines further tightened control over foreign investment starting in 1968/9. This policy change resulted in substantial declines in the country's per capita GDP, with rapid decreases of 41% in 1962 and 23% in 1970, as depicted in panel *a* of Fig. 3.4.

In Malaysia, the government's restrictions on foreign capital and on the local Chinese economy were comparatively less severe than those imposed in the Philippines. Nevertheless, the Malaysian

---

[13] The Warsaw Pact was a defence treaty established by the Soviet Union and its satellite states in Central and Eastern Europe.

[14] The "Filipino First" policy was implemented with the aim of prioritizing Filipino-owned businesses over their foreign counterparts. This policy was originally formulated in response to the effects of free trade and the dominant economic position of the United States in the Philippines after WWII, with the goal of enhancing the role of Filipinos in the national economy. However, it garnered negative reactions from foreign and non-native business communities, particularly from Chinese Filipinos, who felt marginalized in the local economy as a result of this policy. Given the Philippines' status as an agricultural country, its GDP was significantly impacted, as Chinese Filipinos had previously held a major share of the local rice industry.

[15] See, East, William Gordon. 1961. *The Changing Map of Asia: A Political Geography*. London, New York: Methuen.

government, led by Barisan Nasional,[16] introduced provisions in the 1957 Constitution that granted indigenous privileges. These provisions had a significant impact on the local Chinese-led economy. As a result of the prevailing post-war nationalism, by the late 1960s, both Malaysia and the Philippines had been overtaken by Taiwan and South Korea in the catch-up growth phase, as indicated in panel *a* of Fig. 3.4. The decline of the Philippines was particularly evident (also see Fig. 3.2).

In the 1970s, emerging economies across East Asia broadly gained access to industrial technology transfers from Japan. Among these economies, Taiwan and South Korea initiated rapid transitions within this decade. In Southeast Asia, Malaysia achieved a comparable transition record, although its growth performance was significantly influenced by the surges in oil prices during the oil crises of 1973 and 1978. These oil crises were especially impactful on Malaysia's economy during the 1970s, given that oil constituted a substantial portion of Malaysia's non-service exports (panel *a* of Fig. 3.4).

- **The second divergence** in Asia's income transition occurred in the early 1980s, marking a distinct trajectory for the economies of Taiwan, South Korea, and Malaysia (panel *b* of Fig. 3.4). Beginning in the early 1980s, Taiwan and South Korea started the adoption of the second wave of technology diffusion from Japan, progressively transforming from traditional manufacturing industries to technology-based capital-intensive industries (e.g. electronics industry).[17]

In the meantime, Malaysia confronted mounting economic challenges triggered by the global crisis of the early 1980s (1980–1982), which followed its economic boom in the 1970s and placed its oil-dependent economy in jeopardy. The economic instability gave rise to heightened nationalism within the country. Under the authoritarian rule of Mahathir, domestic racial tensions escalated (i.e.

[16] Barisan Nasional is also known as the National Front.

[17] As an example, Taiwan's "Hsinchu Science Park", which served as the cradle of its electronics industry, was established during the second wave of technology diffusion in 1980.

Operation Lalang in 1987),[18] further exacerbating economic stagnation throughout the 1980s. As a result, beginning in the mid-1980s, Taiwan and South Korea accelerated their economic growth, leaving Malaysia significantly behind in the catch-up phase. What distinguishes this second phase of differentiation is the backdrop of the global economic crisis in the early 1980s.

- **The third divergence** emerged in the late 1990s, primarily affecting South Korea and Taiwan, as a consequence of the 1997 Asian financial crisis. In Taiwan, the aftermath of the crisis witnessed a sharp decline in overseas asset prices, prompting domestic capital outflows for investment. Thus, Taiwan's electronics industry began relocating its manufacturing base to mainland China, where labour costs were substantially lower. Consequently, the post-crisis economic conditions hindered the upgrading of Taiwan's local industries, resulting in a phenomenon of a "hollowing out" of the economy. In around 10 years, Taiwan was surpassed by South Korea (see panel *c* of Fig. 3.4).[19]

The experiences of non-resource-based Asian economies demonstrate the significance of economic openness and stability in facilitating rapid catch-up growth and subsequent income transition. Before an economy's successful transformation towards a self-sustaining growth path, access to technology diffusion from the global frontier is a key factor for maintaining the pace of transition. Moreover, the international environment during the catch-up phase is also critical in determining local economic stability, encompassing aspects such as state intervention in crises, enduring relationships with investor countries, and basic state economic policies. An unstable global environment, such as the global financial

---

[18] Operation Lalang was a significant crackdown initiated by the Royal Malaysian Police during October to November 1987. It was ostensibly carried out to pre-empt the outbreak of racial riots in Malaysia.

[19] In Malaysia, the Mahathir government gradually shifted away from its radical nationalism in the early 1990s, particularly in response to the ascension of China on the global stage. The impact of the 1997/1998 Asian financial crisis further compelled the Mahathir regime to relinquish power, leading to the dissolution of the long-dominant conservative political and economic complex associated with the Barisan Nasional regime. Subsequently, the Malaysian economy initiated a recovery phase following the 1997/1998 crisis. See, panel *c* of Fig. 3.4.

crisis, may quickly alter a country's stance towards economic openness, thereby influencing the speed of its transition in the catch-up phase. This dynamic poses a contemporary challenge for developing Asian economies, including China, during their respective paths of economic growth and income transition.

Nevertheless, though growth rate and economic openness determines how long economies will stay in the middle-income category, a process which could be very slow for some economies, it does not prevent an economy from transiting to high-income.

### China's Dual Transition: Lessons from Asian Experiences

Considering the dual economy of Lewis model[20] in Chapter 2, the substantial migration of rural workers contributes to a persistent surplus in the supply of labour for the industrial sector. This surplus exerts a stabilizing effect on industrial wage rates, keeping them fixed and unchanged during the early stages of capital accumulation. However, the situation would alter at the Lewis turning point,[21] where rapid economic growth propels an increase in the demand for industrial labour, breaking the equilibrium in the labour market.

China's demographic and economic development has precipitated a transformation in its labour market equilibrium. If growth of working-age population is considered as a proxy for labour market supply and the change in the number urban employed people as indicative of demand, a distinct reversal in China's labour supply-demand dynamic becomes evident in Fig. 3.5.[22] Notably, this reversal manifested in 2004–2005. Since then, China's annual addition to the labour force showed an irreversible downward trend. This transition to a supplier's market marked China's a fundamental shift in China's labour market dynamics.

[20] See, Lewis, William Arthur. 1954. "Economic Development with Unlimited Supplies of Labour." *The Manchester School of Economic and Social Studies* 22(2): 139–191.

[21] See, Lewis, William Arthur. 1972. "Reflections on Unlimited Labour." In Di Marco, Luis Eugenio (ed.). *International Economics and Development: Essays in Hornor of Raul Prebisch.* New York: Elsevier, pp. 75–96.

[22] In consideration of labour market instabilities stemming from unforeseeable factors, Fig. 3.5 uses 5-year moving average to depict changes in both the working-age population and the number of urban employed people.

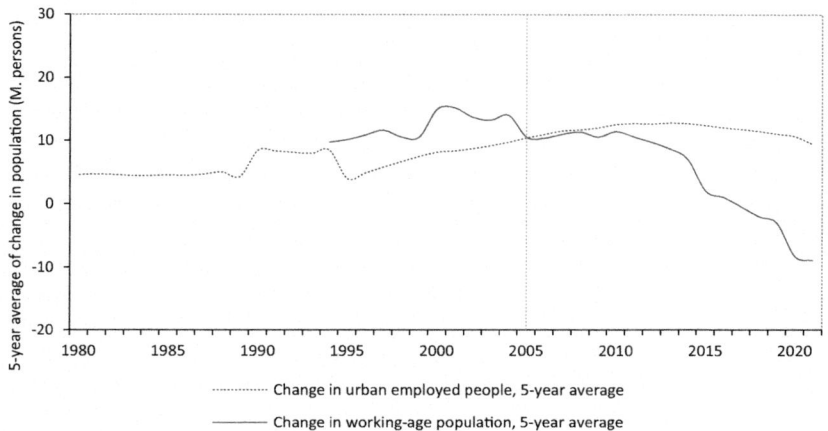

**Fig. 3.5** Supply–demand relationship in China's labour market, 1990–2022 (*Source* National Bureau of Statistics. [n.d.]. *National Data*. Available at https://data.stats.gov.cn/index.htm, accessed 15 August 2023)

Indeed, many Asian economies have undergone comparable experiences in post-war development. Despite China's remarkable economic growth over the last four decades, when the country's labour market underwent a fast demographic transition, its per capita growth remains relatively modest. In 2005, China's elderly population aged 65 and above constituted 7.8% of its total population,[23] marginally surpassing the world average of 7.3%.[24] However, during the same period, China's per capita GDP was only 24.0% of the world average.[25]

[23] National Bureau of Statistics. (n.d.). *National Data*. Available at https://data.stats.gov.cn/index.htm, accessed 15 August 2023.

[24] The World Bank. (n.d.). *World Development Indicators*. Washington: The World Bank. Available at https://datacatalog.worldbank.org/dataset/world-development-indicators, accessed 15 August 2023.

[25] According to the World Bank's World Development Indicator, China's per capita GDP in 2005 was 1753.4 US$ at current price. The same year's World average level was 7293.7 US$. The World Bank. (n.d.). *World Development Indicators*. Washington: The World Bank. Available at https://datacatalog.worldbank.org/dataset/world-development-indicators, accessed 15 August 2023.

It is noteworthy that the reversal of labour market balance does not necessarily signify a reduction in the working-age ratio.[26] Thus, in conjunction with the Lewis turning, another pivotal demographic tipping in economic growth would be the juncture at which the demographic dividend diminishes, signifying the moment when the growth rates of dependent and working-age populations become equal.[27] Technically, this occurrence corresponds to the point when the national dependency ratio undergoes a shift from decline to increase.

Hence, if one defines the initiation of the demographic "gift" as the onset of the dependency ratio plateau (prior to its decline),[28] this juncture in China can be traced to the 1960s (Fig. 3.6). From the 1960s to the early 1980s, the demographic dividend, however, was impeded by China's centrally planned system. In this context, Deng's reform in 1980 should be regarded as the starting point of Chinese economy receiving this demographic "gift". It was not until the year 2010, when total dependency ratio reached its bottom, that China's release of demographic dividend reached its end (Fig. 3.6).

Therefore, although the one-child policy quickly made the Chinese population younger after 1980, it however accelerated China's demographic transition from a high to low dependency ratio within a relatively short timeframe compared to other newly industrialized economies in Asia. From Lewis turning point in 2005 to the conclusion of the demographic dividend in 2010, China's condensed demographic transformations have curtailed the temporal window for economic adjustments in response to the swiftly evolving labour supply dynamics.

As depicted in Fig. 3.7, the period from 2005 to 2010 witnessed a continuous surge in China's working-age population, while the non-working-age population remained stable, primarily due to the diminishing youth dependency under the one-child rule. The concurrent increase in the working-age demographic and their reduced dependency burden significantly contributed to the rapid expansion of China's economic magnitude during the Hu-Wen administration. However, as the adjustment window from Lewis turning in 2005 to the end of demographic

---

[26] See Fig. 2.3 for details.

[27] Williamson, Jeffrey G. 1998. "Growth, Distribution, and Demography: Some Lessons from History." *Explorations in Economic History* 35(3): 241–271.

[28] Ibid.

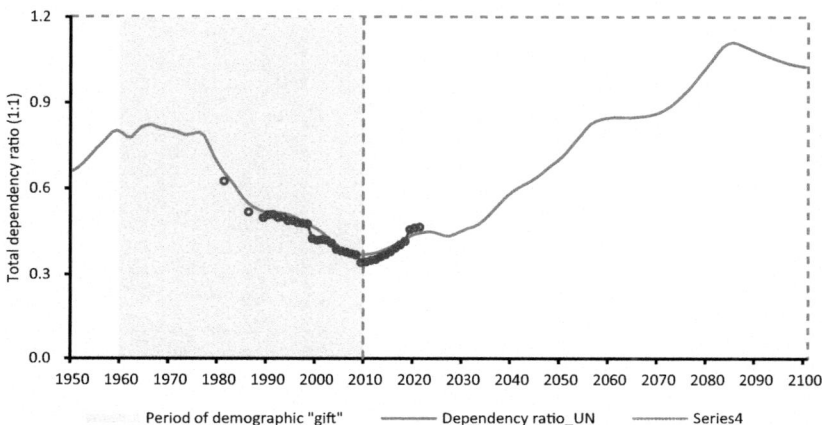

**Fig. 3.6** Total dependency ratio and demographic dividend (*Source* National Bureau of Statistics. [n.d.]. *National Data*. Available at https://data.stats. gov.cn/index.htm, accessed 15 August 2023; United Nations, Department of Economic and Social Affairs, Population Division. 2022. *World Population Prospects 2022*. Available at https://population.un.org/wpp/, accessed 15 August 2023)

dividend in 2010, there was an acceleration in the growth of the elderly population. Consequently, inevitable challenges related to economic growth rates, employment rates and ageing issues emerged.

World industrialization experiences have shown that economic growth has primarily depended on labour input and capital accumulation. However, when the labour market surpasses the Lewis turning point during the transition characterized by a diminishing demographic dividend, the economic growth model encounters challenges in adapting to the deteriorating population structure.

This situation was frequently observed in industrialized economies in East and Southeast Asia after WWII. Japan was the first in experiencing this turning in the early 1960s.[29] Subsequently, towards the end of the

[29] It is widely accepted that Japan's Lewis turning point transpired in the early 1960s. For a detailed calculation of the labour market reversal point, please refer to a collection of works by Ryoshin Minami. See, Minami, Ryoshin. 1968. "Turning Point in the Japanese Economy." *The Quarterly Journal of Economics* 82(3): 380–402; Minami, Ryoshin. 1970a.

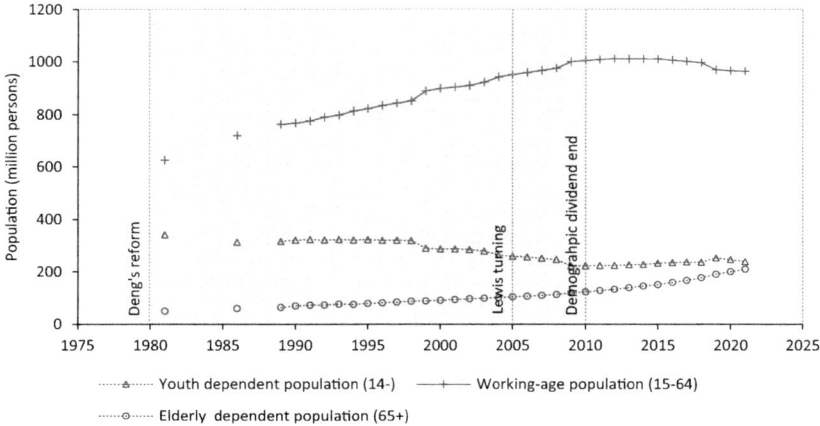

**Fig. 3.7** Turning points in China's labour market: Deng's reform, Lewis turning and the conclusion of demographic dividend (*Source* National Bureau of Statistics. [n.d.]. *National Data.* Available at https://data.stats.gov.cn/index.htm, accessed 15 August 2023; United Nations, Department of Economic and Social Affairs, Population Division. 2022. *World Population Prospects 2022.* Available at https://population.un.org/wpp/, accessed 15 August 2023)

1960s, the four "Asian Tigers"—Taiwan,[30] South Korea,[31] Hong Kong, and Singapore—joined this transformation. As their demographic dividend was fully realized after the Lewis turning point, a notable decrease in labour shortage ensued, significantly impacting the marginal output of capital.

"Further Considerations on the Turning Point in the Japanese Economy (I)." *Hitotsubashi Journal of Economics* 10(2): 18–60; Ryoshin Minami's works of Minami, Ryoshin. 1970b. "Further Considerations on the Turning Point in the Japanese Economy (II)." *Hitotsubashi Journal of Economics* 11(1): 58–122.

[30] Taiwan came to its Lewis turning at the end of the 1960s. See Minami, Ryoshin, and Xinxin Ma. 2014. "Labor Market and the Lewisian Turning Point in China." In Minami, Ryoshin, Fumio Makino, and Kwan S. Kim (eds.). *Lewisian Turning Point in the Chinese Economy*. London: Palgrave Macmillan.

[31] South Korea was argued to reach its Lewis turning point in 1972. For details, refer to Bai, Moo-Ki. 1982. "The Turning Point in the Korean Economy." *The Developing Economies* 20(2): 117–140.

There were two ways to effectively sustain growth momentums in the post-turning transformation phase: (1) Transitioning to an outward economy, thereby liberating capital from constraints imposed by domestic labour productivity and supplies. Examples include Hong Kong and Singapore; (2) Upgrading to labour-saving technologies aimed at enhancing the marginal output of labour. Japan, Taiwan, and South Korea were the case for this approach.

The duration from the Lewis turning point to the conclusion of the demographic dividend spanned approximately 30 years for Japan and 45 years for both Taiwan and South Korea (Fig. 3.8). In contrast, China navigated this period in only five years (Fig. 3.7). As China's dependency ratio has been on the ascent since 2010, its per capita GDP was merely 10.1% of Japan, 23.7% of Taiwan, and 19.7% of South Korea, thereby underscoring China's enduring demographic disadvantage in the ongoing transition.

Furthermore, when juxtaposed with other substantial middle-income countries in Asia, like Malaysia and India, their dependency ratios

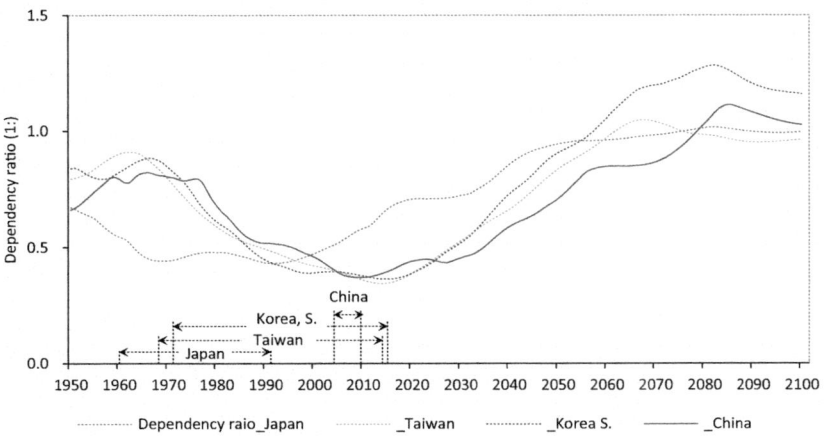

**Fig. 3.8** Demographic turnings among East Asian economies, from Lewis turning to the end of demographic dividend (*Source* National Bureau of Statistics. [n.d.]. *National Data.* Available at https://data.stats.gov.cn/index.htm, accessed 15 August 2023; United Nations, Department of Economic and Social Affairs, Population Division. 2022. *World Population Prospects 2022.* Available at https://population.un.org/wpp/, accessed 15 August 2023)

continue to exhibit a declining trend, expected to be sustained at a low level until the 2050s (Fig. 3.9). In contrast, China's dependency ratio is projected to surpass that of most Asian developing countries in the 2020s. This implies that while Asian developing economies continue to leverage their advantageous demographic structures for another two to three decades, China stands to lose its comparative advantage of low labour cost in global processing trade.

A further comparative analysis of China with its neighbouring developed economies will yield a comprehensive evaluation of China's current position in the income transition in connection to the demographics, aligning it with the growth trajectory observed across East Asia. As previously mentioned, Taiwan and South Korea stand out as the two most recent East Asian economies to have successfully attained high-income status. Consequently, these two economies have been chosen as key points of comparison with China, as illustrated in Fig. 3.10.

In 1986 Taiwan's GDP per capita reached US$10,257 (at constant 2015 prices). After 1986, Taiwan experienced a remarkable six-year period

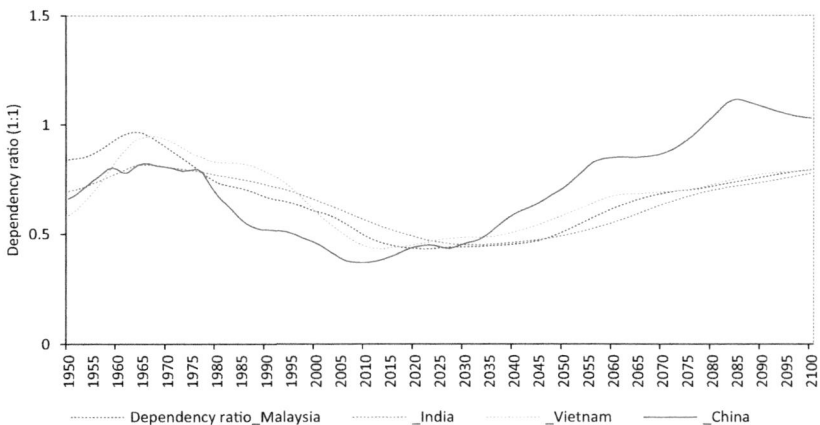

**Fig. 3.9** Dependency ratio in selected middle-income economies in Asia (*Source* National Bureau of Statistics. [n.d.]. National Data. Available at https://data. stats.gov.cn/index.htm, accessed 15 August 2023; United Nations, Department of Economic and Social Affairs, Population Division. 2022. *World Population Prospects 2022*. Available at https://population.un.org/wpp/, accessed 15 August 2023)

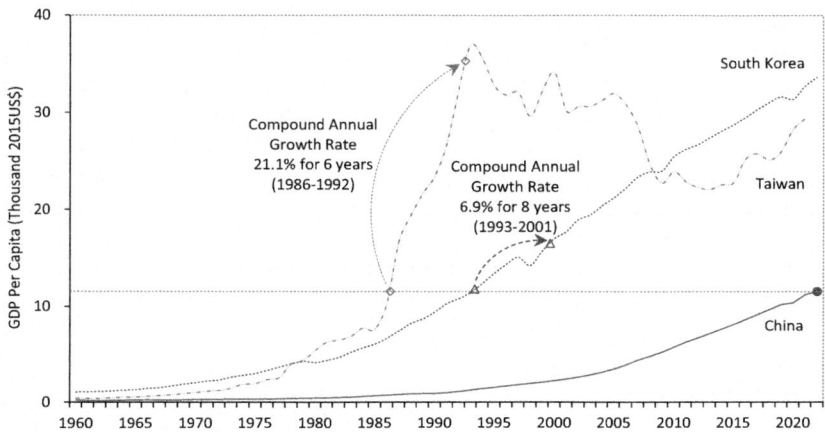

**Fig. 3.10** Per capita GDP (constant price) in South Korea, Taiwan and China, 1960–2022 (*Source* The World Bank. [n.d.]. *World Development Indicators.* Washington: The World Bank. Available at https://datacatalog.worldbank.org/ dataset/world-development-indicators, accessed 15 August 2023; Directorate-General of Budget, Accounting and Statistics of Taiwan. 2022. *Statistical Yearbook of Taiwan 2022.* Available at https://eng.stat.gov.tw/cl.aspx?n=2574, accessed 15 August 2023)

characterized by a compound annual growth rate of 21.1%, propelling it out of the middle-income category. In comparison, South Korea achieved an equivalent level in 1993, with a GDP per capita of US$11,423 at constant 2015 prices. Although South Korea's transition was slightly less rapid than Taiwan's, it continued to exhibit robust growth, registering a compound growth rate of 6.9% from 1993 to 2001. South Korea ultimately attained high-income status in the aftermath of the 1997 Asian financial crisis.

As of 2022, China's per capita GDP has reached a level similar to the level of Taiwan in the mid-1980s and South Korea in the early 1990s. If China's income transition persists at a pace akin to that of South Korea, which represents the most recent successful East Asian economy to ascend to high-income status, it is conceivable that China could achieve high-income status within the next decade.

The World Bank now uses the GNI per capita threshold of US$13,205 to designate an economy as high-income, serving as a benchmark for assessing China's progress towards formalizing its income transition. In this context, as of 2021, China's per capita income stands at US$11,930 (according to the Atlas method), positioning it in close proximity to the high-income entry criterion. Should China's economy sustain a growth rate similar to South Korea's, typically ranging between 6.5 and 7.0% annually, it is conceivable that China could attain high-income status soon. However, as the World Bank's threshold for defining "high income" continues to rise over time, a growth rate of 6.5–7.0% may be considered only moderate in the context of evolving income thresholds. While a potential slowdown in China's growth rate does not necessarily signify a permanent entrapment in the middle-income category, it may result in an extended period of China's presence within this income group should its growth rate decline.[32]

The Chinese government's pre-Covid-19 economic growth target, ranging between 6.5 and 7.0%, aligns with the dynamic and static assessments regarding the ideal growth rate for China's transition from a middle-income to a high-income economy. It becomes evident that China's remarkable four decades of rapid economic growth alone may not suffice for this transition. Instead, the country must undertake comprehensive adjustments and maintain its growth momentum in the near future to expedite its progression beyond the middle-income stage towards high-income status.

Fundamentally, for many large transitional countries, achieving a wholly outward growth pattern proves challenging. In the absence of labour-saving technological changes during the dual transitional window, there would be a significant risk of the economy becoming ensnared in a growth dilemma. China now confronts the peril of succumbing to the

---

[32] In April 2015, Lou Jiwei, the former Minister of Finance, delivered a comprehensive statement at Tsinghua University. He posited that if China were to embark on a path of sweeping reforms, the Chinese economy might sustain a growth rate within the range of 6.5–7.0% in the medium term. However, Lou Jiwei also cautioned that should China fail to seize the opportunity for stimulating growth, it could face a "more than 50 percent chance of falling into the middle-income trap" over the subsequent five to ten years (2020–2025). Importantly, he highlighted the significant impact of population aging on China's transition from middle- to high-income status. For further details, please refer to Lou Jiwei's statement in Lou, Jiwei. 2015. "Qianqi ciji yu dangqian chulu (Early Stimulation and Current Way Out)." *The Paper* published on 1 May 2015. Available at https://www.thepaper.cn/newsDetail_forward_1326853, accessed 15 August 2023.

middle-income trap, given the absence of distinct advantage in either capital or labour returns. This bottleneck encapsulates a critical challenge in China's dual transition.

## DEMOGRAPHIC CHALLENGES TO THE DUAL TRANSITIONS

### *A Cyclical Adjustment or a Structural Downturn?*

The increasing apprehension about China's ability to evade the middle-income trap has garnered public attention. This concern stems from both the deceleration in the country's economic growth since the early 2010s and the economic disruptions caused by the Covid-19 pandemic. Notably, China's real GDP growth rate declined from 6.0% in 2019 to 3.0% in 2022. This implies that China has sustained a period of slower growth, consistently below the 6.5–7.0% threshold, spanning six years since 2016.

As the Chinese government's Zero-Covid policy (*qing ling zhengce*)[33] has taken its toll on previously accessible sources of growth, China now confronts the challenge of identifying fresh avenues for economic expansion. The concerns expressed by the Chinese populace regarding the "trap" in the ongoing income transition underscore the nation's uncertainty about whether the post-Covid-19 economic stagnation is a transient or enduring phenomenon.

Prior to the present circumstances, China experienced two prior downturns in per capita growth in 1989 and 1998. The first was attributed to late 1980s price liberalization ( *jiage chuangguan*),[34] while the latter was

---

[33] Distinct from the strategy of "living with Covid-19", the Zero-Covid policy constituted a public health measure aimed at achieving stringent control and maximal suppression of Covid-19 during the pandemic within China. This policy entailed the implementation of severe mobility restrictions, including the complete closure of cities and interregional transportation networks. It is noteworthy that the Zero-Covid policy was not without significant economic ramifications for China, particularly within the service sector during periods of lockdown. These consequences have become increasingly apparent, extending into China's manufacturing sector, where they manifested as a proliferation of bankruptcies and a protracted recovery period following the cessation of Zero-Covid measures, which occurred towards the end of 2019.

[34] Price liberalization refers to a significant economic reform undertaken by the Chinese government in 1988/1989. This reform was aimed at addressing various economic challenges inherent in dual-track price system ( *jiage shuanggui zhi*) by permitting market forces to determine product prices. As a consequence, there was a widespread and substantial increase in the prices of numerous products, a trend that extended from the late 1980s into the early 1990s.

linked to the 1997/1998 Asian financial crisis.[35] Some analysts argue that the ongoing downturn is cyclic in nature, citing reasons such as global economic contraction and insufficient investment to stimulate growth. Conversely, a substantial portion of experts opine that China's current sluggish economic performance is indicative of a structural downturn that followed the Covid-19 pandemic. This perspective is grounded in macroeconomic considerations. On the demand side, a relatively low share of household income in GDP necessitated China's reliance on an unusually high level of state investment in infrastructure and the housing sector. Nevertheless, the rapid growth observed in both domains appears to have reached its culmination.

In 2012, the Chinese economy had also come to a point where the share of manufacturing in GDP had reached its peak and where the service sector is increasingly important in GDP contribution (Fig. 3.11).[36] Nevertheless, it presents a formidable challenge for the service sector to sustain double-digit growth rates, a feat well within the capabilities of the manufacturing sector. Today's China has already reaped most of the advantages stemming from its low labour costs and expansion in low-end industries for exports.

It would be difficult for Chinese economy to be primarily driven by domestic consumption as the white goods industry, automotive sector, and housing industry had sequentially reached their growth plateaus. On the supply side, China's total factor productivity (TFP) has experienced deceleration,[37] attributable in part to the impending labour shortage arising from the ongoing demographic transition.

In contrast to other income transitions observed in East and Southeast Asia, as previously discussed, China's demographic shift is poised to have

---

[35] The 1997/1998 Asian financial crisis had a profound impact on several East and Southeast Asian nations during the late 1990s. The crisis originated in Thailand and swiftly propagated to neighbouring countries, triggering a ripple effect that stoked concerns of financial contagion spreading throughout Asia.

[36] In 2012, the service sector's contribution to China's GDP stood at 45.5%, surpassing that of the industrial sector, which accounted for 45.4%.

[37] According to the *Penn World Table*, China's TFP exhibited a slowdown commencing in 2017, registering at 0.42. After its recent peak in 2017 (at 0.43), productivity experienced a rapid decline, reaching 0.40 just before the onset of the Covid-19 pandemic. For more detailed data, please refer to Groningen Growth and Development Centre. 2021. *Penn World Table Version 10.0*. Available at http://www.rug.nl/ggdc/productivity/pwt, accessed 15 August 2023.

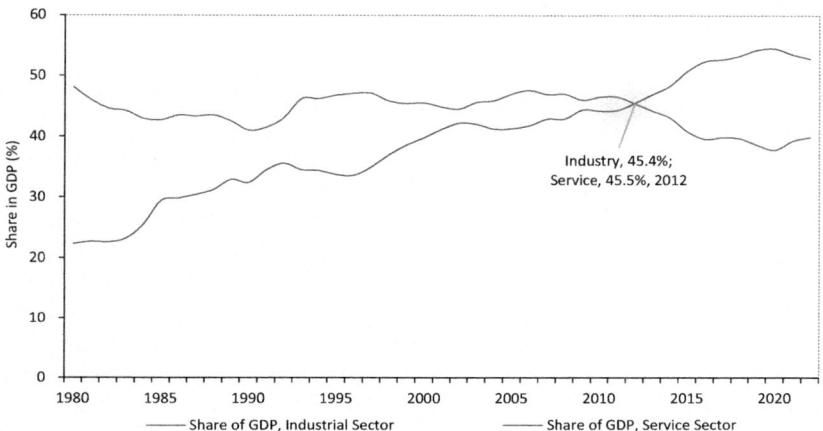

**Fig. 3.11** GDP distribution across the industrial and service sectors in China, 1980–2002 (*Source* National Bureau of Statistics of China. [n.d.]. *Zhongguo tongji nianjian* (*China Statistical Yearbook*). Beijing: China Statistics Press)

an enduring influence on its income transition process. This impact manifests in various ways, including the contraction of domestic markets, the erosion of economies of scale in production, and the fiscal repercussions associated with heightened age-related expenditures and escalating dependency ratios. These challenges[38] loom large in today's China, exerting significant influence on the nation's ongoing transition towards achieving high-income status.

---

[38] The economic ramifications of demographic change are multifaceted, when coupled with the process of income transition. They encompass the immediate responses of the domestic economy to population decline. The OECD (2016a, 2016b) has underscored several significant economic consequences arising from declining populations, including an escalating burden on pension systems, a diminishing labour supply, a reduction in the tax base, a contraction in labour stock, and a decrease in domestic market consumption. For a more comprehensive understanding of these effects, please refer to OECD. 2016a. *OECD Pensions Outlook 2016*. Available at https://www.oecd-ilibrary.org/finance-and-investment/oecd-pensions-outlook-2016_p ens_outlook-2016-en, accessed 15 August 2023; OECD. 2016b. *Better Ways to Pay for Health Care*. Available at https://www.oecd-ilibrary.org/social-issues-migration-health/ better-ways-to-pay-for-health-care_9789264258211-en, accessed 15 August 2023.

## Challenges to Income Transitions

On a positive side, there are expectations that the population decline observed in China's most densely populated regions could potentially lead to opportunities for more lenient land utilization, reduced congestion, decreased housing expenses, and, to a certain extent, diminished environmental stress. While numerous outcomes remain uncertain, the certain economic impacts are already being experienced.

The most evident and immediate challenges include a diminishing labour supply and an escalating total dependency ratio. Although the total population remains substantial, the working-age population has already commenced an absolute decline in recent years and has been decreasing as a proportion of the overall population over an extended period. The proportion of older age groups within the working-age population has been steadily increasing in China, foreshadowing a forthcoming elevation in the total dependency ratio.

China has recently implemented a more relaxed birth control policy, permitting all families to have up to three children. This adjustment may lead to an increase in the number of children over the long term. Concerning the child-dependency ratio, as of 2022, there are more than four individuals for every one person below the age of 15. Projections suggest that this ratio is expected to decline to 3.9 by the year 2060, despite a rapid escalation in the burden of elderly dependency.[39]

While these figures do not account for the contributions of older Chinese individuals who continue to actively participate in the workforce, the fact remains that Chinese workers will face a mounting burden if the country is to maintain growth in per capita GDP, elevate per capita living standards, and transition into the high-income category, all while coping with the substantial growth of the inactive population. Given that China is currently undergoing an unprecedented contraction in its working-age ratio, a phenomenon rarely observed in its history, a sharp decline in the labour force is now underway.

Returning to the comparison of China's demographic circumstances with those of East Asian countries during their transition periods, it is important to note that China's recent decline in the working-age population is not an isolated occurrence. In fact, both South Korea and

---

[39] OECD. (n.d.). *Historical Population Data and Projections (1950–2050)*. Available at https://stats.oecd.org/index.aspx?DataSetCode=POP_PROJ, accessed 15 August 2023.

Japan have undergone a similar trajectory, moving from high post-war fertility rates to very low fertility levels and an overall decrease in population. Figure 3.12 illustrates the dynamics of demographic changes in the context of income transitions for China, Japan, and South Korea.

Japan achieved upper-middle-income status in 1968 and transitioned to high-income status in 1977, accomplishing this feat before its young and middle-aged working-age population began to age. Similarly, South Korea reached upper-middle-income status in 1988, and its robust economic growth during that period was largely attributable to the rapid expansion of its young and middle-aged workforce and a low dependency ratio. Both Japan and South Korea evolved into aging societies; however, by the time they attained this demographic shift, they had already ascended to high-income status. In contrast, China finds itself in a different situation.

As early as the 1980s, when the one-child policy took effect, Wu Cangping forecasted that China would encounter significant demographic challenges, foreseeing a scenario where the country might "get older

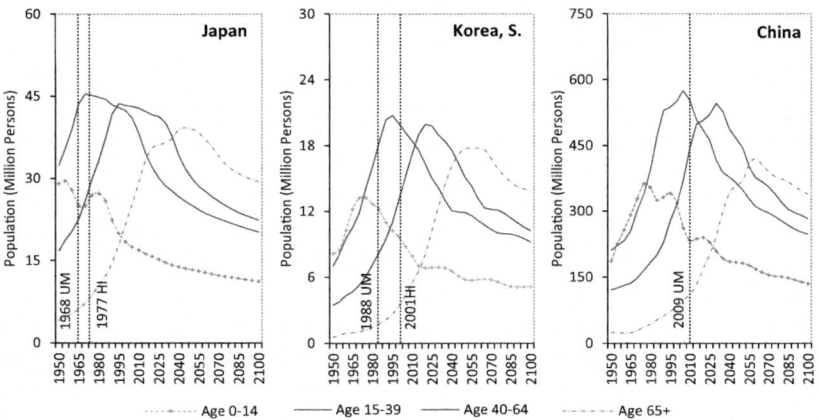

**Fig. 3.12** Dynamics of working age population in Japan, South Korea and China (million persons) (*Note* "UM" standards for the upper-middle-income threshold, whereas "HI" stands for high-income. *Source* United Nations, Department of Economic and Social Affairs, Population Division. 2022. *World Population Prospects 2022*. Available at https://population.un.org/wpp/, accessed 15 August 2023)

before getting rich". By the time China achieved upper-middle-income status in 2009, the proportion of its young and adult population aged 15–39 had already surpassed its zenith, as depicted in Fig. 3.12.

China is now experiencing the onset of population aging, and this demographic change carries significant implications. The reduction in population size threatens to deprive China of the advantages associated with economies of scale, particularly in labour-intensive industries crucial for its export-led growth. The impact of an aging population and a diminishing workforce on the Chinese economy, particularly at a stage where the country is still in the process of development, has become a source of serious concern for its leadership.

## CHINA'S ONGOING DEMOGRAPHIC TRANSITION

### Growth-Induced Population Structural Change

The experiences of some Asian economies suggest that China's economic growth potential is likely to witness a sharp decline as its demographic dividend diminishes. Moving forward, the primary driver for future growth is expected to hinge on technological progress and improvements in TFP.

Under the Hu-Wen administration, China's growth was propelled not primarily by a fundamental increase in labour productivity but rather by extensive capital investments. Beyond the coastal areas, substantial government-led investments in central and eastern regions also suffered increased industrial productivities, enabling these regions to catch up with their costal counterparts. This suggests that central and western China may persist in contributing to national growth by capitalizing on their advantages in labour-intensive industries.

China's total population has experienced significant growth over the period from 1962 to 2021, doubling in size to reach a population of 1.4 billion in 2021.[40] However, starting in the late 1990s, the population growth rate underwent a rapid decline. Projections indicated that the total population was expected to peak between 2020 and 2030, as illustrated in Fig. 3.13. This demographic change was primarily driven by China's stringent family planning policies and the resulting decline

---

[40] National Bureau of Statistics. (n.d.). *National Data*. Available at https://data.stats.gov.cn/index.htm, accessed 15 August 2023.

in birth rates, a trend further accelerated by the Covid-19 pandemic. Consequently, China's total population began to decline in 2022.[41]

In addition, the decline in the total population will be preceded by a contraction in the working-age population. Projections indicate that the proportion of the population aged 15–64 is expected to decrease from 72.4% in 2015 to 57.3% in 2060. The share of young and middle-aged labour, individuals between the ages of 20 and 45, in the population has already been on a rapid decline and is projected to continue diminishing, dropping from 48.3% in 2015 to an anticipated 34.4% in 2060.

In 2022, China's median age reached 38.4 years, in stark contrast to the global median age, which is estimated to be just over 30 years by the Central Intelligence Agency (2023).[42] According to current projections, China's population is expected to decline by approximately 10% from the present time until 2060. Moreover, the elderly population (aged 65 and above) is expected to account for well over one-third of the population

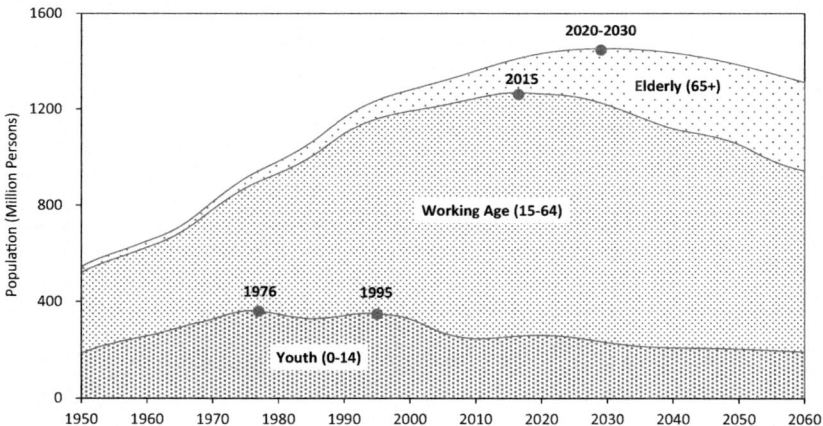

**Fig. 3.13** Chinese population and age structure (*Source* OECD. [n.d.]. *Historical Population Data and Projections (1950–2050)*. Available at https://stats. oecd.org/index.aspx?DataSetCode=POP_PROJ, accessed 15 August 2023)

---

[41] The National Bureau of Statistics has reported that China's total population began to decline in 2022, decreasing from 1.413 billion in 2021 to 1.412 billion in 2022.

[42] The Central Intelligence Agency. 2023. *The World Factbook*. Available at https://www.cia.gov/the-world-factbook, accessed 15 August 2023.

by the end of this projection period. This demographic change is set to fundamentally reshape both the structure of China's population and its labour supply.

China's rapid demographic transformation and the concurrent shrinking of its working-age population can be primarily attributed to low fertility rates (Fig. 3.14). The TFR in China experienced a sharp decline in the late 1960s and much of the 1970s, plummeting from a peak of 7.5 (in 1963) during the baby boom of the 1960s, a period when Mao Zedong encouraged childbirth. Subsequently, from the 1970s to 1990s, the TFR in China gradually decreased from above six to approximately replacement levels at 2.1–2.2, before further declining to 1.2 in recent years.

The decline in fertility rates in China has occurred simultaneously with a significant increase in life expectancy (illustrated in Fig. 3.14), rising from 33.3 years in 1960 to 78.2 years in 2022. This improvement in life expectancy has allowed China to maintain overall population growth even after the TFR fell below the replacement rate. Despite substantial changes

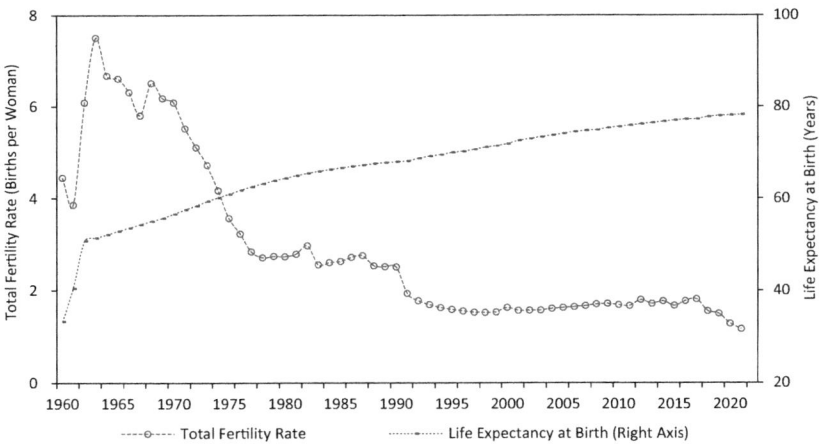

**Fig. 3.14** Longevity and fertility in China (*Source* The World Bank. [n.d.]. *World Development Indicators*. Washington: The World Bank. Available at https://datacatalog.worldbank; National Bureau of Statistics of China. [n.d.]. *Zhongguo renkou he jiuye tongji nianjian* (*China Population and Employment Statistics Yearbook*). Beijing: China Statistics Press)

in China's social welfare system (e.g. advancements in the medical care system), the recent implementation of two-child and three-child policies may potentially contribute to an increase in the overall dependency ratio among the working-age population in China.

One direct consequence of the rising dependency ratio is a decline in labour mobility.

### *Growth-Induced Population Displacement*

In 2022, with a population of 1.4 billion, China stands as the world's second-most populous country,[43] and ranks third in terms of land area. While China's population density is not as high as in some other East Asian economies, like Japan, a significant portion of China's population resides in regions that are considerably denser than the national average.[44] In fact, over 40% of China's population lives in areas that collectively make up just above 10% of the country's total territory.

The 1952–2022 data reveals a consistent trend of population concentration in eastern and southeastern coastal regions of China. Population growth has been particularly rapid around Beijing and, to a somewhat lesser extent, in the vicinity of Shanghai and the eastern coastal areas. This phenomenon is closely tied to the lower fertility rates typically observed in economically advanced regions.

Thus, the population growth observed in China's economically advanced regions primarily stems from interregional migration rather than natural population increase. The higher population density and growth in these areas between 1952 and 2022 can be attributed to the influx of people from surrounding large cities, with this trend becoming notably more pronounced after 2004/2005. However, in general, a larger proportion of Chinese regions are now experiencing net population outflows. These demographic changes have significant implications, particularly in provinces that serve as a labour-sending or receiving area.

---

[43] India is expected to become the world's most populous country in 2023. The projected total population of India for this year is expected to reach 1.43 billion people, surpassing China's population of 1.41 billion.

[44] Many people in China reside in areas characterized by population densities exceeding 500 individuals per square kilometres. For instance, Shanghai's population density surpasses 3,926 persons per square kilometres. This concentration of population in urban centres is a pattern shared with other East Asian economies and is particularly prominent in the Yangtze River Delta and Zhujiang Delta.

This is particularly pertinent because it is typically the younger population who are more inclined to move, and they are the most affected by dependency issues.

High population concentration presents both advantages and disadvantages. China's economic performance, especially its export-led growth since the early 2000s, has been largely facilitated by the availability of rural migrant workers. As a result of over four decades of interregional labour migration, a significant portion of the working-age population now resides in major cities. Consequently, rural regions that traditionally supplied these labour forces face challenges, particularly in meeting the labour demands for local labour-intensive agricultural production. This shortage of agricultural labour is especially acute in the regions surrounding large cities in the east and southeast coastal areas of China, where fertile land is abundant.

The ongoing demographic transition in China appears to further accentuate the existing settlement pattern, characterized by a stark contrast between densely populated urban areas and sparsely populated rural regions. Since the mid-1980s and throughout much of the 1990s, China's rural areas have witnessed significant out-migration, driven largely by rural migrant workers seeking employment in cities, particularly in the industrial sector, where they can secure better wages. While the post-2010 economic slowdown and the 2020–2022 Zero-Covid measures have somewhat diminished the demand for migrant labour in urban industries along the coastal areas, they have not fundamentally altered the intersectoral labour flows.

The decline in labour supply in rural China has been steadily accelerating, with an average annual population change of −0.9% in the years 1980 to 2022. This trend intensified after the 1994 market reform, with an average annual change of −1.5% observed from 1994 to 2022. Since most of the labour outflow comprises young and middle-aged individuals, the labour conditions in rural areas continue to deteriorate. Despite the implementation of various social policies aimed at improving conditions in rural areas, such as enhancements to the rural pension system and healthcare,[45] the dominant nationwide trend remains one of ongoing rural-to-urban migration.

[45] Martins, Joaquim Oliveira, and Christine de la Maisonneuve. 2006. "The Drivers of Public Expenditure on Health and Long-Term Care: An Integrated Approach." *OECD Economic Studies* 43(2): 115–154.

It not only influences the future supply of labour in the market but also bears implications for the effectiveness of the two-child policies. The migrant population has demonstrated a positive response to these policies,[46] highlighting the potential for positive outcomes that may offset negatives, which could have been overlooked by China's nationwide non-differential population policies. This underscores the importance of considering China's substantial interregional demographic variations when formulating and implementing policies. The reason is China's great interregional differences in demographics.

## REGIONAL DIFFERENCES IN DEMOGRAPHICS

### Northeast China

Based on tabulation of China's 2020 population census,[47] the provincial population structure in China reveals notable patterns. China's less economically developed regions, including inland provinces, tend to exhibit higher dependency ratios, while economically advanced areas generally have lower dependency ratios. Interestingly, there seems to be a decreasing gap in dependency ratios as urbanization continues to progress in China. Based on the insights from Fig. 3.15, regions can be classified into three major groups.

- Regional dependency ratios in highly urbanized area (i.e. Beijing, Shanghai, Zhejiang, Guangdong, and Tianjin) are notably lower, averaging around 26.7%. This means that for every 100 working-age people, there are approximately 27 young and elderly dependents.
- In the intermediate provinces situated around the national level, the dependency ratio tends to stabilize at around 31.5%.
- However, in Henan, Guangxi, and Guizhou, the average dependency ratio experiences a sudden increase, reaching 36.0%. Henan records the highest, at 36.6% according to the 2020 census.

---

[46] The next chapter will delve into the subject matter in greater depth.

[47] Here data are collected from the Office of the Leading Group of the State Council for the Seventh National Population Census. 2022. *China Population Census Yearbook 2020*. Beijing: China Statistics Press. Available at http://www.stats.gov.cn/sj/pcsj/rkpc/7rp/indexch.htm, accessed 15 August 2023.

Notably in Fig. 3.15, the lowest dependency group encompasses not only the wealthiest regions in China but also economically less prosperous provinces in the northern (i.e. Qinghai, Shanxi, and Inner Mongolia) and northeastern (i.e. Liaoning, Jilin, and Heilongjiang) parts of the country. Unlike Beijing, Tianjin, and Shanghai, the northeast's low dependency ratio is primarily a result of its abundant labour stock, rather than being solely driven by economic affluence. This highlights the significance of labour force composition and availability as a key factor influencing dependency ratios across different regions in China.

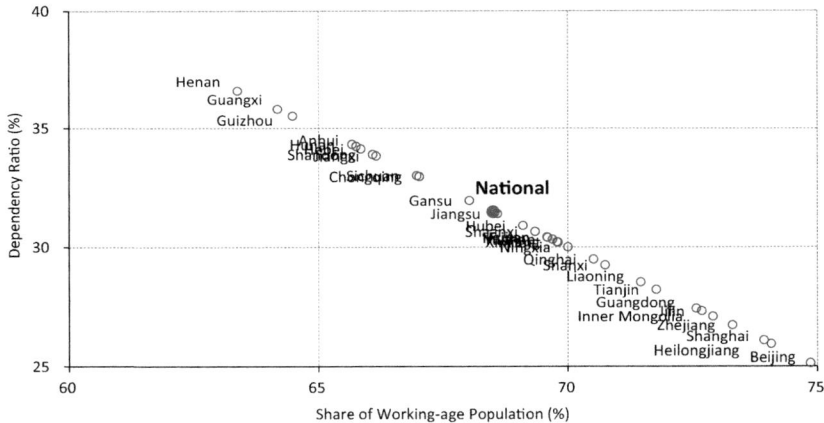

**Fig. 3.15** Regional labour stock and dependent ratio in China (*Note* This figure uses the dependency ratio as a tool to depict the regional labour market structure. The dependency ratio is a metric that quantifies the number of dependents, encompassing individuals aged 0–14 and 65+, in relation to each person aged 15–64. It serves as an age-population ratio, indicating the proportion of individuals who are not part of the labour force (the non-productive segment) to those actively engaged in the labour force (the productive segment). In this figure, the dependency ratio takes into account both elderly and child dependencies, offering insights into the collective burden placed on the productive population. *Source* Office of the Leading Group of the State Council for the Seventh National Population Census. 2022. *China Population Census Yearbook 2020.* Beijing: China Statistics Press. Available at http://www.stats.gov.cn/sj/pcsj/rkpc/7rp/indexch.htm, accessed 15 August 2023)

Indeed, the northeast region of China has experienced population growth rates below the national average, attributed to its declining birth rates since the 1990s. While the northeast region does contribute a significant portion of migrant labour, with many migrants heading to Beijing and its surrounding areas, the scale of this labour flow from the northeast is comparatively small when compared to the substantial labour migration from central to eastern coastal China. Hence, without the presence of either a large-scale labour outflow or a rapid population increase, the population in northeast China has generally remained stable since the 1980s.

The labour lock-in experienced in the northeast region is not a result of industrial underdevelopment in the area. Historically, the development of the northeast region occurred over a similar time span as that of other regions in the country. Partly as a consequence of this historical development, the northeast has enjoyed favourable conditions, including a more advantageous man-land ratio compared to the rest of China. In essence, the factors contributing to labour lock-in in this region are more complex and multifaceted, encompassing demographic trends, economic dynamics, and patterns of labour migration.

In the first decade following the economic reforms, the northeast region remained a crucial industrial hub in China. Workers in the northeast commanded higher salaries than their counterparts in many of the eastern coastal provinces. For instance, by the year 1992, Liaoning's per capita GDP was as high as that of Guangdong.[48] During the early stages of the post-reform era, the northeast region benefited from the persistence of the planning system, which was still operational at that time. Additionally, it provided a higher level of social welfare, which factored into the compensation packages for workers. As a result, the relatively higher salaries served as a potent incentive for workers to stay in the region. Unlike the large-scale labour migration that was occurring from central China to the east coast, the situation in the northeast represents an exceptional case in China's regional labour flow and demographic transition, shaped by a combination of economic and social factors.

---

[48] In 1992, the per capita GDP in Liaoning amounted to 3,693 yuan, whereas in Guangdong, it stood at 3,698 yuan per person. For the relevant data, please refer to National Bureau of Statistics of China. (n.d.). *National Data*. Available at https://data.stats.gov.cn/english/easyquery.htm?cn=C01, accessed 15 August 2023.

## Inland China

Being at the forefront and primary beneficiaries of economic opening up, the coastal areas of China have been magnets for an influx of migrant workers from inland China. However, since the early 2010s, the growth momentum of coastal provinces has started to decelerate as their local economies reached advanced stages in China. This slowdown in development in coastal areas has coincided with a declining trend in labour inflows, subsequently leading to rising labour costs in these regions.

It is widely accepted that sufficient labour supply was one of the lynchpins of coastal China's fast development. With the fast economic growth in coastal regions, young and middle-aged adult labourers moved from central China to these economically advanced areas, which had the effect of depleting the local economies of their regions of origin. This phenomenon is particularly true in some western and southwestern provinces, where there is now a low labour stock to support child and elderly dependents.

As a result of labour outflows, inland China exhibits a relatively lower working-age ratio (Fig. 3.15). Nevertheless, the region's labour stock remains substantial compared to coastal areas. Inland China has maintained a consistently high population size of individuals aged 15–64, while coastal areas have experienced a decline since the early 2010s. The relatively lower living standards and resulting lower labour costs in inland China have made it a choice for investors seeking to capitalize on cheaper labour. Inland China's fixed asset investment in the manufacturing sector has surged, particularly when its total labour stock rebounded in the mid-2000s. This suggests that manufacturers, especially those producing labour-intensive goods, may have started moves inland to take advantage of labour cost savings.[49]

Rather than solely depending on the industrial upgrading of the coastal regions, relying on inland China's economic integration and adoption of practices from coastal areas seems a more viable strategy for future growth. There is also a pressing need to significantly increase investment in human capital development in the inland regions. However, a significant challenge lies in educating the vast inland population to

---

[49] For instance, Foxconn, a large electronics manufacturer, has relocated a part of its manufacturing operations to inland areas such as Zhengzhou, Chengdu and other interior places.

acquire the skills required for adopting advanced industrial technology from the coastal areas. If local human capital investment cannot be enhanced quickly, it could impede the further development of inland regions. Consequently, human capital development and labour supply have the potential to become constraints on China's manufacturing sector as it moves inland. Addressing these challenges is crucial to ensure the successful transition and sustained growth of industries in inland China.

## DEMOGRAPHIC IMPLICATIONS FOR THE CHINESE ECONOMY

At the national level, demographic analysis is instrumental in understanding and addressing the challenges posed by socio-economic impacts for policymaking purposes. Developing nationwide strategies will be crucial for China to effectively address these challenges and navigate its demographic transition. These strategies will play a vital role in shaping the country's economic and social policies to ensure sustainable development and the well-being of its population in the face of demographic changes.

Maintaining the sustainability of public finances is a significant policy concern for China. Achieving this goal involves not only reforming expenditures that are strongly influenced by demographic changes (i.e. pensions and healthcare), but also enhancing the efficiency of service delivery across the country. While the pension reforms implemented in the past decade have contributed to ensuring the long-term sustainability of pension provision, there remains substantial work to be done in this regard. Ongoing efforts and reforms will be necessary to address the challenges posed by China's changing demographics and to secure the stability of public finances in the future.

In agriculture, the aging rural population and the migration of working-age labour to other industries have compelled some rural households to discontinue agricultural production. While the outflow of rural labour in past decades prompted the adoption of labour-saving technologies in Chinese agriculture, the aging of the rural population will soon have an impact on production, particularly as the experienced older generation approaches retirement age. This presents a potential threat to China's agricultural development.

In China's secondary industry, there have been notable decelerations in export-oriented sectors that traditionally depended on an ample and cost-effective labour force. The diminishing working-age population and the rapidly rising dependency ratio have affected China's competitive edge in exporting labour-intensive goods, resulting in reduced capital inflow from foreign investors in certain instances. Achieving deeper industrialization is of particular importance for China's future growth. The accessibility to capital inflows and cutting-edge technologies from economically advanced nations holds the potential to boost productivity, foster efficiency gains, and create opportunities for innovation. This can be pivotal in further enhancing China's competitiveness on the global stage, strengthening its position in international economies.

On the demand side, the phenomenon of population aging presents enormous opportunities in certain sectors like medicine and finance, primarily owing to the higher savings rates among older individuals. However, an aging society has shown a propensity for reduced levels of innovation and entrepreneurship. The elderly population is less likely to actively contribute to future developments that involve higher levels of associated risk, often preferring activities that yield immediate returns, such as salaried employment. Therefore, there exists the possibility that the elderly demographic may displace younger individuals from skilled positions, compelling the younger generations, who are in their prime years, to engage in lower-end jobs. This dynamic could have unfavourable implications for the Chinese economy.

While foreign labour may help fill certain skill gaps, this policy inclination diverges from immigration policies implemented in smaller economies like Hong Kong and Singapore. Nevertheless, it is improbable that the Chinese government would heavily depend on this foreign labour source, as it could significantly alter the country's demographic landscape.

Returning to the fundamental aspects, as per the neoclassical growth theory, a country's production and growth are primarily determined by two foundational factors: capital and labour. Within the same technological framework that diffused from developed countries following WWII, disparities in demographics partly shape a country's growth trajectory and development outcomes. In China's case, these disparities are predominantly a result of its stringent population control policies. A careful examination of China's labour structure projection, based on empirical studies, indicates that the country is poised to face substantial challenges stemming from its historical population policies over the past four decades. China's economic transition serves as an illustrative example of a growth path constrained by labour under the evolving complexities of demographic conditions. While these characteristics significantly contributed to China's economic transformation from the 1980s to the 2000s, the impending decline in the country's working-age ratio during the 2020s to 2030s is likely to pose increasing difficulties for its ongoing income transition.

In many post-war transitional countries, income transitions always coincide with demographic transitions. Thus, it is often challenging to establish an ideal labour market institution during these countries' economic transitions, including that in China. Therefore, China's labour market is characterized by a relatively complex population structure, primarily resulting from the government's strict regulation of births and fertility since the inception of economic reforms. In essence, while the population structure has consistently influenced labour market supply, the demand for labour has, in turn, intermittently impacted intersectoral and interregional labour mobility, ultimately compelling the government to reconsider its long-standing family planning policy.

The examination of China's dual transition in this chapter provides valuable insights into China's demographic dynamics within the context of its rapid income growth. The interplay between demographic and income transitions will play a key role in shaping China's future growth trajectory, with the labour market serving as a proxy to comprehend the changes in China's comparative advantages or disadvantages in the global distribution of industrial processing.

Demographic transition is indeed a protracted process. Similarly, the effects of population policies require considerable time to manifest and contribute to socio-economic development. The future development of China hinges on the efficacy of its policies, particularly in mitigating the immediate repercussions of its shrinking working-age population. Therefore, the subsequent chapter (Chapter 4) endeavours to establish links between the effectiveness and ineffectiveness of government's population policies by examining the birth responses of different labour/population segments to China's two-child policies.

# REFERENCES

Bulman, David, Maya Eden, and Ha Nguyen. 2017. "Transitioning from Low-Income Growth to High-Income Growth: Is There a Middle-Income Trap?" *Policy Research Working Paper* No. WPS 646. Washington, DC: World Bank.

Directorate-General of Budget, Accounting and Statistics of Taiwan. 2022. *Statistical Yearbook of Taiwan 2022.* Available at https://eng.stat.gov.tw/cl.aspx?n=2574, accessed 15 August 2023.

East, William Gordon. 1961. *The Changing Map of Asia: A Political Geography.* London, New York: Methuen.

Felipe, Jesus, Utsav Kumar, and Reynold Galope. 2014. "Middle-income Transitions: Trap or Myth?" *Asian Development Bank Economics Working Paper Series* No. 421. Available at www.adb.org/sites/default/files/publication/149903/ewp-421.pdf, accessed 15 August 2023.

Groningen Growth and Development Centre. 2021. Penn World Table Version 10.0. Available at http://www.rug.nl/ggdc/productivity/pwt, accessed 15 August 2023.

Im, Fernando Gabriel, and David Rosenblatt. 2013. "Middle-Income Traps: A Conceptual and Empirical Survey." *Policy Research Working Paper* No. WPS 6594. Washington, DC: World Bank.

Levesque, Moren, and Maria Minniti. 2006. "The Effect of Aging on Entrepreneurial Behavior." *Journal of Business Venturing* 21(2): 177–194.

Lou, Jiwei. 2015. "Qianqi ciji yu dangqian chulu (Early Stimulation and Current Way Out)." *The Paper* published on 1 May 2015. Available at https://www.thepaper.cn/newsDetail_forward_1326853, accessed 15 August 2023.

Martins, Joaquim Oliveira, and Christine de la Maisonneuve. 2006. "The Drivers of Public Expenditure on Health and Long-Term Care: An Integrated Approach." *OECD Economic Studies* 43(2): 115–154.

National Bureau of Statistics of China. (n.d.). *National Data.* Available at https://data.stats.gov.cn/english/easyquery.htm?cn=C01, accessed 15 August 2023.

National Bureau of Statistics of China. (n.d.). *Zhongguo tongji nianjian (China Statistical Yearbook).* Beijing: China Statistics Press.

OECD. 2016a. *OECD Pensions Outlook 2016.* Available at https://www.oecd-ilibrary.org/finance-and-investment/oecd-pensions-outlook-2016_pens_outlook-2016-en, accessed 15 August 2023.

OECD. 2016b. *Better Ways to Pay for Health Care.* Available at https://www.oecd-ilibrary.org/social-issues-migration-health/better-ways-to-pay-for-health-care_9789264258211-en, accessed 15 August 2023.

OECD. (n.d.). *Historical Population Data and Projections (1950–2050).* Available at https://stats.oecd.org/index.aspx?DataSetCode=POP_PROJ, accessed 15 August 2023.

Office of the Leading Group of the State Council for the Seventh National Population Census. 2022. *China Population Census Yearbook 2020*. Beijing: China Statistics Press. Available at http://www.stats.gov.cn/sj/pcsj/rkpc/7rp/ind exch.htm accessed 15 August 2023.

The Central Intelligence Agency. 2023. *The World Factbook*. Available at https://www.cia.gov/the-world-factbook, accessed 15 August 2023.

The World Bank. (n.d.). *World Bank Atlas Method—Detailed Methodology*. Available at datahelpdesk.worldbank.org/knowledgebase/articles/378832-what-is-the-world-bank-atlas-method, accessed 15 August 2023.

The World Bank. (n.d.). *World Development Indicators*. Washington: The World Bank. Available at https://datacatalog.worldbank.org/dataset/world-development-indicators, accessed 15 August 2023.

United Nations, Department of Economic and Social Affairs, Population Division. 2022. *World Population Prospects 2022*. Available at https://population.un.org/wpp/, accessed 15 August 2023.

World Bank. 2022. *World Bank GNI Per Capita Operational Guidelines and Analytical Classifications*. Available at http://databank.worldbank.org/data/download/site-content/OGHIST.xls, accessed 15 August 2023.

Wu, Cang-ping. 1986. "Theoretical Explanations of the Rapid Fertility Decline in China." *Population Research* 3(3): 16–23.

# CHAPTER 4

# Connecting the Effectiveness and Ineffectiveness of the Two-Child Policies

**Abstract** This chapter presents an empirical investigation into the inter-regional disparities in China's birth rate responses following the relaxation of the one-child policy. This chapter reveals that, subsequent to the policy change in 2013, China's regional variations in birth intentions and fertility rates have exhibited significant differences. Notably, these interregional birth disparities among different families have not resulted in a substantial overall **increase** in births. This phenomenon can be attributed to two primary factors: first, the rapid urbanization process has increased the affordability of rural populations to have additional children, and second, it has simultaneously led to a reduction in the population segment characterized by higher fertility intentions, in conjunction with income growth in urban areas.

**Keywords** One child policy · Two child policy · Birth rate · Rural migrant workers · Cyclical unemployment · Structural unemployment · Urbanisation · Population displacement

© The Author(s), under exclusive license to Springer Nature Switzerland AG 2024
J. Du, *China's Labour Market, 1950–2050*, Palgrave Studies in Economic History, https://doi.org/10.1007/978-3-031-53138-5_4

# The Narrowing Time Window
## for Population Policies

### *Declining Fertility Rates and the Shrinking Child-Bearing Age Female Population*

After the relaxation of the one-child rule in 2013,[1] a modest rebound in the national birth rate occurred in 2014. However, in 2015, the birth rate decreased to an even lower level. Figure 4.1 illustrates the age-specific birth rate responses to the Chinese government's two-child policies for all women of childbearing age in China.

Two factors could have contributed to this phenomenon.

- Firstly, the conditional two-child policy implemented in 2013 applied solely to individuals born in the 1980s, excluding the majority of couples born before the one-child policy.
- Secondly, a significant share of women of childbearing age had already given birth during the auspicious Year of the Dragon in 2012.[2]

As the conditional two-child policy did not reach expected effect, the government implemented a universal two-child policy in 2015,[3] applicable to all couples. This policy change led to noticeable responses in birth rates. As depicted in panel *a* of Fig. 4.1, while the fertility rates of women generally increased after the introduction of the 2015 universal two-child

---

[1] See, Chinese Communist Party Central Committee, Document No. 15. 2013. "Zhonggong zhongyang guowuyuan yinfa guanyu tiaozheng wanshan shengyu zhengce de yijian (Opinions Issued by the CCP Central Committee and the State Council on 'Adjusting and Improving the Family Planning Policy')." Beijing: 30 December 2013.

[2] The most favoured zodiac sign in Chinese culture is the dragon. In societies characterized by collectivism, there is a widespread belief that individuals born under the dragon zodiac sign possess qualities such as honesty and bravery. Furthermore, it is often believed that the life of a "dragon" baby is predestined for success and affluence.

[3] Chinese Communist Party Central Committee, Document No. 40. 2015. "Zhonggong zhongyang guowuyuan guanyu shishi quanmian lianghai zhengce gaige wanshan jihua shengyu fuwu guanli de jueding (Decision of the Central Committee of the CCP and the State Council on Implementing the Universal Two-Child Policy and Reforming and Improving the Management of Family Planning Services)." Beijing: Chinese Communist Party Central Committee, 31 December 2015.

policy, the birth rate among women aged 20 to 24 declined shortly thereafter. This suggests that the relaxation of the one-child policy had minimal impact on individuals in their early twenties. Interestingly, women in the age groups of 30 to 34 and 35 to 39 exhibited positive responses to the policy relaxation, albeit to a modest extent.

Ten years before the implementation of two-child policies, the fertility desires of women of childbearing age exhibited two prominent features shown in Fig. 4.1:

- Older age groups displayed greater desires for fertility, and this trend became notably pronounced following the introduction of the universal two-child policy.
- Despite the short-term increase in fertility rates achieved by the two-child policies, the overall trend in fertility desires among women of childbearing age has experienced a comprehensive decline over the past decade.

In reality, these phenomena can be attributed to the following factors:

- The fertility of older age group women was previously constrained and delayed by the one-child policy when they were in their younger years.
- The relatively higher household income and stable employment prospects have instilled greater financial confidence in them to consider having an additional child.

As a result, by 2019, the two-child policies primarily influenced the fertility decisions of women born in the 1980s and the late 1970s. For younger women, the two-child policies did not have a significant impact on their fertility desires related to having their first child.

These features align with the neoclassical perspective on the inverse relationship between fertility rates and economic growth.[4] Despite the

---

[4] For example, Becker, Gary S. 1981. *A Treatise on The Family*. Chicago: Harvard University Press; Becker, Gary S. 1964. *Human Capital: A Theoretical and Empirical Analysis, with Special Reference to Education*. New York: Columbia University Press; Becker, Gary S. 1976. *The Economic Approach to Human Behaviour*. Chicago: University of Chicago Press; Schultz, Theodore W. 1963. *Economic Value of Education*. New York: Columbia University Press.

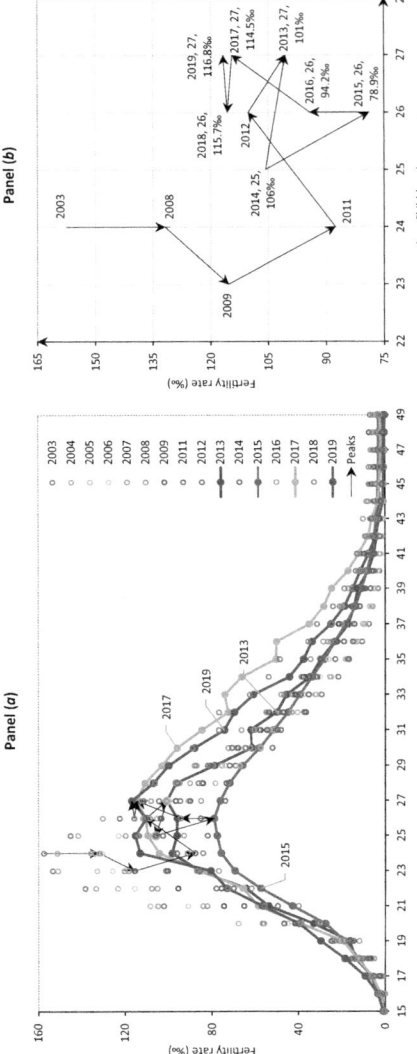

**Fig. 4.1** Fertility rate among different age groups in China before Covid-19, 2003–2019 (*Note* Given the uncertainties caused by the Covid-19 pandemic and the implementation of the Zero-Covid policy, this figure is limited to data up to the year 2019. This choice allows us to concentrate on assessing the mere impact of the two-child policies on the Chia's birth rate change *Source* National Bureau of Statistics of China. (n.d.). *Zhongguo renkou he jiuye tongji nianjian* (*China Population and Employment Statistics Yearbook*). Beijing: China Statistics Press)

Chinese government's policy changes, which initially allowed couples to have two children and later expanded to permit up to three children as of 2021, several factors have collectively influenced Chinese couples' decisions on expanding their family size. These factors include the historical legacy of fertility control, escalating living expenses, and the growing burden of supporting an aging population.

Besides the change in fertility intention and the time required for population policies to manifest their effects, the efficacy of these policies is contingent upon the composition of the female population,[5] often referred to as the base population within the country. When the demographic structure of women of childbearing age undergoes rapid changes, the timing of population policy implementation can substantially influence both its cost and effectiveness. Table 4.1 provides an overview of the female population structure in China, while Fig. 4.2 illustrates the evolving fertility behaviours among various age groups of women.

In general, there has been a rapid decline in the number of women of childbearing age following the implementation of the one-child policy (Table 4.1). Specifically, the size of the post-90s female population has contracted by a significant 19.0% when compared to that of the post-80s cohort. Furthermore, the post-00s generation, comprising the offspring of individuals from the post-70s and 80s, has experienced an even more pronounced decline, with a reduction of a quarter in population size compared to a decade earlier. Over the past decade, there has been a general decrease in fertility behaviour across all age groups of women in China.

The current increase in births in China is mainly driven by women born in the 1990s, particularly those in their 20s and 30s (panels *a*, *b* of Fig. 4.2). While the fertility rate among the post-85s cohort is relatively low, their significant population base continues to contribute to the overall increase in births, as shown in panel *a* of Fig. 4.2. However, in the coming decade, the post-00s generation will replace the post-90s as the largest contributors to population growth. This shift suggests that the impact of population-encouraging policies may diminish over time, as the post-80s and 90s cohorts, despite their large population base, are expected to lose fertility by then.

---

[5] Miller, Amalia R. 2011. "The Effects of Motherhood Timing on Career Path." *Journal of Population Economics* 24(3):1071–1100.

**Table 4.1**  Distribution of women in fertile age groups in China

| Year of Birth | Proportion of Female Population in Total Population by Age Group (‰) | | | | | Estimated Female Population (Million Persons) | Decade-On-Decade Change Rate (%) |
| | 2015 (1) | 2016 (2) | 2017 (3) | 2018 (4) | 2019 (5) | (6) | (7) |
| --- | --- | --- | --- | --- | --- | --- | --- |
| 1950–1954 | 5.4 | 5.3 | 5.3 | 5.2 | 5.7 | 31.3 | Post-50s |
| 1955–1959 | 5.8 | 5.7 | 5.7 | 5.6 | 5.0 | 32.2 | – |
| 1960–1964 | 6.8 | 6.7 | 6.6 | 6.8 | 8.3 | 40.8 | Post-60s |
| 1965–1969 | 8.6 | 8.6 | 8.5 | 8.5 | 8.8 | 50.0 | +39.5% |
| 1970–1974 | 8.8 | 8.7 | 8.7 | 8.6 | 7.9 | 49.5 | Post-70s |
| 1975–1979 | 7.1 | 7.1 | 7.0 | 7.0 | 6.7 | 40.4 | +2.8% |
| 1980–1984 | 7.2 | 7.1 | 7.0 | 7.1 | 7.4 | 41.5 | Post-80s |
| 1985–1989 | 8.7 | 8.8 | 8.7 | 8.6 | 8.8 | 50.6 | +0.3% |
| 1990–1994 | 7.4 | 7.4 | 7.3 | 7.3 | 6.2 | 41.3 | Post-90s |
| 1995–1999 | 5.8 | 5.4 | 5.5 | 5.3 | 4.9 | 31.1 | -19.0% |
| 2000–2004 | 4.6 | 4.8 | 4.7 | 4.7 | 4.8 | 27.3 | Post-00s |
| 2005–2009 | 5.0 | 5.0 | 5.1 | 5.0 | 5.0 | 29.1 | -23.8% |
| 2010–2014 | 5.5 | 5.5 | 5.4 | 5.2 | 5.1 | 31.0 | Post-10s |
| 2015–2019 | – | – | – | – | 5.4 | 37.9 | +22.1% |

*Note* To assess the immediate impact of the two-child policies on China's birth rate change, Table 4.1 and Fig. 4.2 utilize five-year averages spanning from 2015 to 2019 for the size of age-specific female groups. The data pertaining to the "proportion of group female population in total population" in columns (1) to (5) has been sourced from the annual *China Population and Employment Statistics Yearbook*. The size of the female population in different age groups is estimated based on the proportions provided in columns (1) to (5) and the total population data from 2015 to 2019, which are gathered from the *China Statistical Yearbook*. This Table is further developed from Du, Jane. 2017. "China's Population Policy and the Future of Its Labour Market." In Tong, Sarah Y., and Jing Wan. (eds.). *China's Economy in Transformation under the New Normal*. Singapore: World Scientific

*Source* National Bureau of Statistics of China. (n.d.). *Zhongguo renkou he jiuye tongji nianjian* (*China Population and Employment Statistics Yearbook*). Beijing: China Statistics Press; National Bureau of Statistics of China. (n.d.). *Zhongguo tongji nianjian* (*China Statistical Yearbook*). Beijing: China Statistics Press

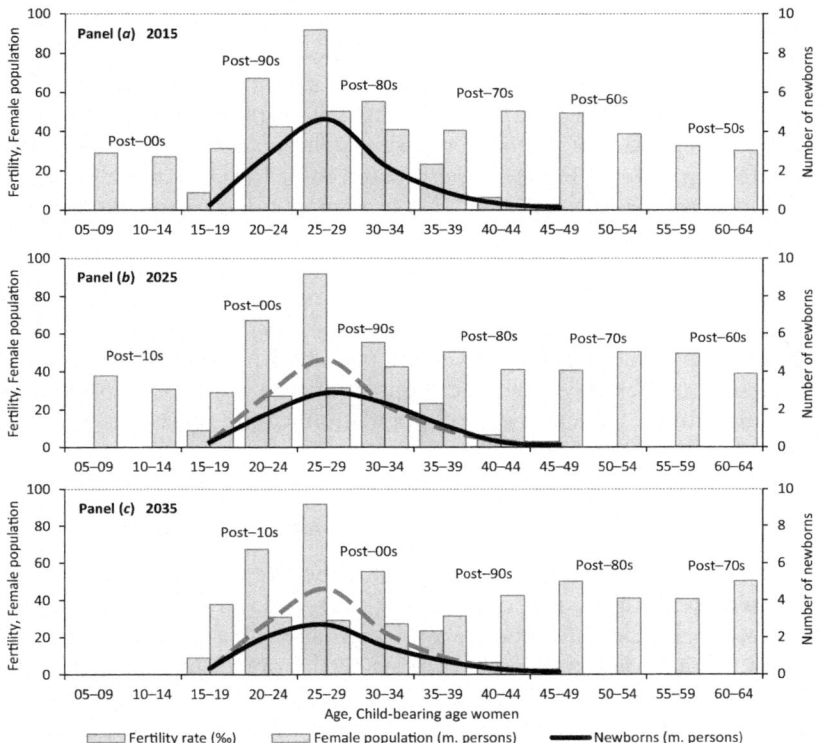

**Fig. 4.2** The changing effects of the two-child policies, 2015–2035 (*Note* The fertility rates following the implementation of the two-child policies have been calculated as average estimates derived from the 2015–2017 national population sample surveys as reported in the *China Population and Employment Statistics Yearbook*. The sizes of the female population within various age groups are estimations derived from the results presented in Table 4.1. This figure is an updated version of Du, Jane. 2017. "China's Population Policy and the Future of Its Labour Market." In Tong, Sarah Y., and Jing Wan. (eds.). *China's Economy in Transformation under the New Normal*. Singapore: World Scientific. *Source* National Bureau of Statistics of China. (n.d.). *Zhongguo renkou he jiuye tongji nianjian* (*China Population and Employment Statistics Yearbook*). Beijing: China Statistics Press; National Bureau of Statistics of China. (n.d.). *Zhongguo tongji nianjian* (*China Statistical Yearbook*). Beijing: China Statistics Press)

While the size of the female population born in the 2010s has rebounded to the level of the post-90s cohort, predicting fertility rates among this group remains uncertain. Even if one assumes that fertility rates will remain consistent over the next 20 years, projecting to 2035, the expected impact of population easing policies based on the post-10s generation (panel *c* of Fig. 4.2) is estimated to be lower than that in 2025 (based on the post-00s cohort). This is primarily due to the expectation that fertility rates in the future are likely to be generally lower than those in the present.

Consequently, the smaller population base of females from the post-00s (of childbearing age) is unlikely to counteract the impending decline in labour supply. This suggests that if the two-child policies fail to leverage the advantage offered by the larger population size of the post-90s generation, the future effectiveness of population easing measures may be curtailed (panel *b*, *c* of Fig. 4.2).

### *Effects of Two-Child Policies Beyond the Mid-2030s*

Over time, a variety of factors, including the preference for a leisurely and childless lifestyle, the opportunity cost and direct expenses associated with childbearing, and delayed marriage, have jointly influenced couples' fertility desires. Merely relaxing birth control measures is insufficient to return China's birth rate to the levels observed prior to the implementation of the one-child policy. However, the transition from the one-child policy to the two-child policies is anticipated to contribute to the long-term expansion of China's labour force.[6]

---

[6] In terms of population size, if the one-child policy had remained in place, the population was expected to reach its peak at approximately 1.40 billion around the year 2023. However, with the implementation of the two-child policies, China's population is projected to peak at 1.45 billion in 2029. These estimations align with the findings of Zeng and Wang's (2014) and are consistent with the projections of the United Nations. In reality, China's population began to decline in 2022, primarily due to the unexpected changes in family decision-making resulting from the Covid-19 pandemic and the country's stringent Zero-Covid policy enforced between 2020 and 2022. Zeng, Yi, and Zhenglian Wang. 2014. "A Policy Analysis on Challenges and Opportunities of Population/Household Aging in China." *Journal of Population Aging* 7: 255–281.

- Regarding fertility rates: Following the relaxation of the one-child policy, the fertility rate for second children among women of child-bearing age exhibited an immediate increase in 2014, albeit for a brief duration before experiencing a subsequent decline. This decline was accompanied by a continuous decrease in the fertility rate for first children. As a result, China's overall fertility rate among women of childbearing age decreased by 3.1%.[7] By 2015, the fertility rate for second children had reverted to the 1999 level of 1.2%.
- Regarding labour stock: China's labour force, comprised of individuals aged 18 to 64, exhibited a gradual decline throughout the 2010s. Projections indicate that this trend is expected to continue with a moderate decrease in the 2020s until the mid-2030s. However, there is no significant divergence in labour force trends between the one-child and two-child policies during this period.

After the 2030s, the cumulative impact of the two-child policies is expected to result in a significantly larger labour force in China compared to what would have been the case under the one-child policy. Projections indicate that by 2040, there could be an additional 30 million individuals in the labour force, and this number is expected to further increase to 60 million by 2050. Therefore, while the effectiveness of China's two-child policies remains uncertain, any potential benefits are likely to manifest in the labour market after the mid-2030s. This implies that even if these policies succeed in increasing China's labour supply, it will take approximately 18 to 20 years for the newborns to enter the job market.

Indeed, China's labour market has undergone significant changes in recent years. The rapid economic growth and the expansion of higher education have led to the accumulation of human capital in the country. While this has contributed to overall economic development, it has also presented challenges, particularly concerning the shortage of skilled labour in certain industries. As the share of labour with tertiary education increases, the issue of worker shortages in industrial sectors has become more serious. Therefore, in addition to the concerns about the

---

[7] The fertility rate of childbearing-age women is defined as the average number of children that would be born per female aged 15 to 49 within a specific period. This differs from the TFR, which represents the number of children each female would have if all females lived to the end of their childbearing years and gave birth according to the age-specific fertility rates for that particular area and time period.

overall fertility rate not meeting expectations, addressing the underlying regional fertility gap is crucial. The primary objective of the two-child policies is to alleviate the impending labour shortage in China's labour market. Consequently, an important question is whether the current labour market conditions could influence the rate and distribution of the newly added labour force, and how this, in turn, could impact China's ongoing transition to a high-income economy. This complex interplay between demographic transition and labour market dynamics is a critical aspect of China's economic development.

## Structural Changes in Employment

China's working-age ratio peaked in 2010 and has since experienced a gradual annual decline. If one considers yearly growth rate of the working-age population as a proxy for new labour market supplies and the yearly employment growth in the urban sector as the demand, it becomes evident that China's labour supply has consistently fallen short of meeting demand for many years, as indicated earlier in Fig. 3.5.

In a broad context, there is a common presumption that a slowdown in economic growth often leads to elevated rates of unemployment. Nevertheless, before the adoption of China's Zero-Covid policies, the Chinese government revealed that in 2018, urban areas saw the creation of 13.6 million new job opportunities. Furthermore, official reports indicated that the registered urban unemployment rate was at 3.8%, while the surveyed urban unemployment rate stood at 4.9%, reflecting a marginal decreased of 0.1% compared to the preceding year 2017.

During this period, China witnessed an unprecedented surge in the number of new college graduates, reaching a record high of 8.2 million individuals. Simultaneously, the population of "long-distance" migrant workers expanded to 173 million. Consequently, the quest for employment in the urban sector became intensely competitive. The deceleration of economic growth generated concerns regarding potential job losses. However, the Chinese government's official announcement, which emphasized the sustained stability of unemployment rates over several years, seemed to alleviate apprehensions among the Chinese populace.

Contrary to conventional expectations, the question arises as to why the overall unemployment rate, including the youth unemployment rate, did not exhibit an increase within the context of a decelerating economy.

There are three types of unemployment, namely.

- Cyclical Unemployment: This is contingent upon economic fluctuations, particularly business cycles. During economic downturns or recessions, businesses may reduce their workforce, resulting in a rise in cyclical unemployment. Conversely, during periods of economic growth, this type of unemployment typically decreases.
- Frictional Unemployment: This type of unemployment arises from individual circumstances, such as job seekers transitioning between jobs or entering the labour market for the first time. It is often considered temporary and typically occurs due to the time lag in finding suitable employment.
- Structural Unemployment: This is the result of a mismatch between the skills possessed by the labour force and the skills demanded by the job market. It is caused by fundamental economic changes, such as shifts in technology or industry, and tends to have long-lasting effects on unemployment rates.

The first type of cyclical unemployment usually affects industrial workers and often serves as the primary driver of high unemployment rates in developing countries. In the context of China, urban citizens in China are relatively less affected by cyclical unemployment, primarily due to household registration (*hukou*) restrictions and the country's urban–rural dualistic economic structure. Thus, cyclical unemployment has a significant impact on rural migrant workers. For instance, during global financial crises that have affected the Chinese economy, a contraction in demand has compelled many migrant workers to return to their rural homes. Conversely, when the economy experiences a recovery phase, labour shortages become prevalent. Notably, nationwide shortages of migrant workers in the years 2004 and 2009 exemplify the typical consequences of cyclical unemployment in China. These instances underscore the cyclical nature of labour demand in economic sectors and its direct impact on the employment status of rural migrant workers, who often play a key role in industrial and urban labour markets.

However, the challenges faced by urban Chinese are the latter two types—structural and frictional unemployment.[8] Structural unemployment, in particular, is distinctive due to its basis in fundamental economic

---

[8] The structural and frictional unemployment together constitute natural unemployment.

changes and its propensity to persist over an extended period. Both the registered and surveyed unemployment rates, as reported in official documents, are calculated based on the urban population. Thus, their combined statistical significance closely aligns with the natural unemployment rate. China's registered unemployment rate has consistently maintained stability over time. The most significant fluctuation occurred between 4.0% in 2002 and 4.3% in 2003, which transpired prior to the onset of the Covid-19 pandemic.

It is asserted that economic growth remains a primary political goal for the Chinese government. Thus, sustained growth in the Chinese economy is expected to result in the creation of new job opportunities. However, the attainment of full employment is contingent upon the intricate dynamics of labour demand and supply, especially given the labour market reaching the Lewis turning point in 2005, with increased industrial positions to accommodate labour supplies. The realization of full employment hinges on the specific segmentation of labour demand and supply. Unemployment, fundamentally, is the discrepancy between real economic growth and the optimal potentials of the economy. Therefore, the prevalence of structural and frictional unemployment is deemed more commonplace than cyclical unemployment[9] due to ongoing structural economic adjustments.

Despite the Chinese government's assurances of a stable labour market, worries regarding unemployment are growing. The empirical evidence in China has substantiated this inference. As is shown in Fig. 4.4, the registered unemployment rates for individuals in their teens to the early twenties have consistently exceeded the national average. Since 2018 youth unemployment rates have displayed on a persistent upward trend. In other words, the employment challenges faced by college graduates have been just as significant as those encountered by rural migrant workers in China's labour market (Fig. 4.3).

---

[9] Cyclical unemployment is frequently elucidated through Okun's Law. Okun provided a benchmark analysis establishing a correlation between alterations in a country's unemployment rate and changes in its real economic growth rate. See, Okun, Arthur. 1962. "Potential GDP: Its Measurement and Significance." American Statistical Association *Proceeding of the Business and Economic statistics Section*: 98–104.

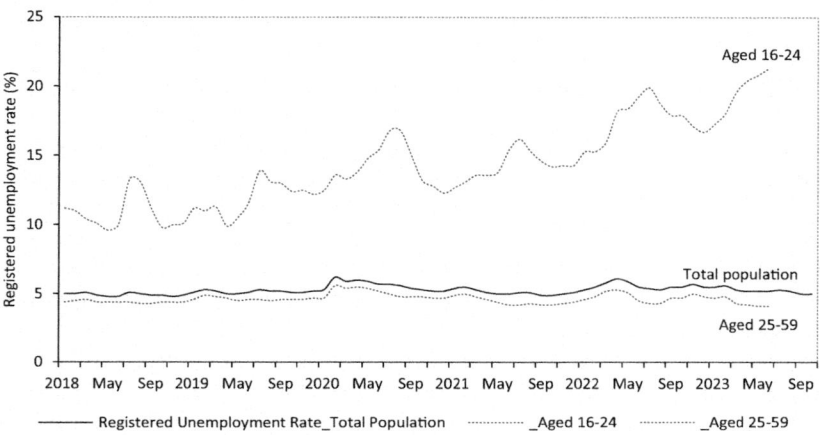

**Fig. 4.3** Monthly registered unemployment Rate since 2018 (*Source* National Bureau of Statistics. (n.d.). National Data. Available at https://data.stats.gov.cn/index.htm, accessed 15 August 2023)

### *Rural Migrant Workers*

An influential factor that has exerted a substantial impact on China's labour market since the economic reforms is the wage gap between sectors and regions, complementing the country's abundant labour supply. The considerable wage disparity, both between rural and urban areas and between inland and coastal regions, has played a pivotal role in directing low-wage labour towards the industrial sector. This phenomenon has expedited China's rapid economic transition.

Over the course of 40 years of labour market transformation, the number of intersectoral labourers—rural migrant workers—has reached its zenith[10] (also see Fig. 2.4). Moreover, just before the onset of the Covid-19 lockdown in China, during the years 2018 to 2019, migrant

[10] Cai, Fang, and Meiyan Wang. 2005. "Challenge facing China's Economic Growth in Its Aging but not Affluent Era." *China and World Economy* 14: 20–31.

workers witnessed an apparent wage increase,[11] surpassing the country's GDP growth rates by 6.5 to 6.8%.[12] Attracting labour inflows by raising wage levels became increasingly challenging for China's industrial sector.[13]

According to the 2020 National Population Census, in urban regions, the ratio of migrant inflows to local household registered population was 0.6 in 2020 for the working-age group (Fig. 4.5, Panel a). Within the 25–34 age group, the same distribution ratio reached its highest point at 0.8, with interprovincial male labour inflows surpassing those of females (Fig. 4.5, Panel b). This implies that the probability of distant migration is greater among young rural labourers, particularly males. This demographic pattern has served as an advantage in maintaining a relatively young urban population through interregional labour flow.

While the substantial migration of rural labourers to urban areas has contributed to a younger urban Chinese population, it has concurrently led to a shortage in labour input in agriculture. Meanwhile, the increasing returns on land have heightened the opportunity cost for rural labourers to engage in urban sector employment, thereby exerting upward pressure on the wage rate of migrant workers since 2005.

[11] According to *Migrant Workers Monitoring Survey Report*, during the period of 2018 to 2019, the wages of migrant workers witnessed an apparent increase, with an overall growth rate ranging from 6.5 to 6.8%. Within the construction industry, specifically, the wage growth was even more significant, ranging from 7.4 to 8.5%. These findings indicate that labour costs in the industrial sector experienced a comprehensive rise due to the constraints in labour market supply. For more detailed information, please refer to Tables 5 in *Migrant Workers Monitoring Survey Report of 2018 and 2019*. National Bureau of Statistics of China. 2020. *Migrant Workers Monitoring Survey Report 2019*. Available at http://www.stats.gov.cn/sj/zxfb/202302/t20230203_1900710.html, accessed 15 August 2023. National Bureau of Statistics of China. 2019. *Migrant Workers Monitoring Survey Report 2018*. Available at http://www.stats.gov.cn/sj/zxfb/202302/t20230203_1900299.html, accessed 15 August 2023.

[12] China's GDP growth rate in 2018 and 2019 were 6.7% and 6.0% according to *World Bank's World Development Indicators*. On average lower than wage increase of migrant workers in the same period. See, the World Bank. (n.d.). World Development Indicators. Washington: The World Bank. Available at https://datacatalog.worldbank.org/dataset/world-development-indicators, accessed 15 August 2023.

[13] Wang, Dewen, Fang Cai, and Wenshu Gao. 2006. "Globalization and the Shortage of Rural Workers: A Macroeconomic Perspective." In: Ingrid Nielsen, Russell Smyth and Marika Vicziany. (eds.). *Globalization and Labour Mobility in China*. Clayton: MAI Press.

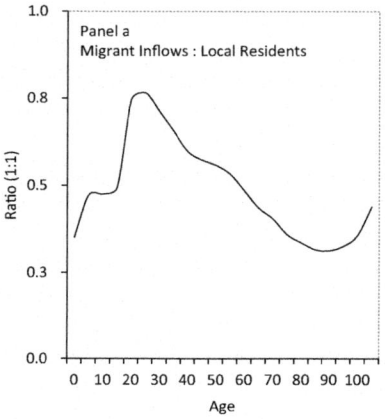 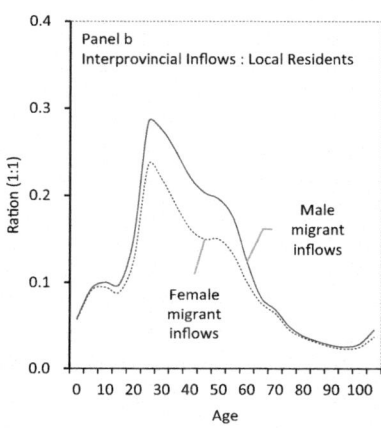

**Fig. 4.4** Ratio of migrant inflows to local registered residents by age groups, 2020 population census (*Source* Population Census Office of the State Council, and the Department of Population and Employment of the National Bureau of Statistics of China. 2022. *Tabulation of Population Censuses of People's Republic of China 2020.* Beijing: China Statistics Press)

Under current conditions, the quantity of rural migrant workers and their wage levels have displayed a consistent annual increase. This persistent upward trend in wages among migrant workers gives rise to concerns regarding the sustainability of industrial wage growth. Should industrial wages continue to rise in an attempt to draw in labour input, there is a risk that China's industrial competitiveness may be compromised due to the accompanying rise in labour costs. This situation underscores the delicate balance that China must navigate to ensure both ample employment opportunities and sustained industrial competitiveness within a dynamic economic environment.

### College Graduates

The employment challenges faced by college graduates differ significantly from those faced by rural migrant workers. When the first wave of college students from the expanded university enrolment entered the labour market, unemployment among college graduates became increasingly common. From the perspective of human capital accumulation, college graduates are evidently in an advantageous position; but whether their skills align with market need is a separate consideration. Moreover, with the rapid diminishment of the demographic dividend and a deceleration in economic growth, China is confronted with a heightened risk of cyclical unemployment. Economic downturns can lead to job losses, especially in industries sensitive to economic fluctuations. Therefore, unlike rural migrant workers, college graduates are susceptible not only to cyclical unemployment but also to structural unemployment.

Age-disaggregated statistics reveal that the highest unemployment rate[14] was observed within the 16–24 age group (Fig. 4.4), signifying that the employment prospects for new college graduates were more challenging compared to the working-age population in general. Furthermore, the constancy of China's overall unemployment rate implies that well-educated young individuals entering the labour market are not effectively integrating. This misalignment between labour skills and market demand raises concerns about the efficient utilization of China's existing labour force, particularly in light of the impending labour shortage in the near future.

When China's labour market structure weakens, several consequences unfold. The marginal return to labour is likely to slow down and, in some cases, decline. The two major groups in today's labour market—migrant workers and college graduates—have generated significant impacts on Chinese economy. This not only reduces the efficient labour supply but also strain China's social welfare systems.

### Pension System

China's demographic dividend was most pronounced when the country's working-age ratio reached its peak in 2010.[15] After 2010, employment in China began to shift towards the service industry. A common characteristic of people engaged in the service industry is their unstable payment ability to contribute to social security funds. Many non-industrial employers and employees are reluctant to participate in national insurance due to the job instability and high pension fees. Consequently, the

---

[14] Cai, Fang, and Kam Wing Chan. 2009. "The Global Economic Crisis and Unemployment in China." *Eurasian Geography and Economics* 50(5):513–531.

[15] The absolute number of working-age population peaked at approximately one billion in 2013.

amount of social security funds paid by people newly entering the social security system has decreased compared to before.

As of 2022, China has 150 million migrant workers, a majority of whom live and work in the urban sector. Without urban household registration, migrant workers are often not covered by China's social insurance system. This exposes the risks that migrant workers have faced in today's labour market.

Raising the pension eligibility age is a strategy that can effectively alleviate fiscal burdens while simultaneously increasing the labour force participation. Presently, China's retirement age is set at 60 for men and 50 for women, which is relatively low in comparison to the global trend of increasing retirement ages, typically ranging between 60 and 65. This argument has garnered strong support for the proposal to raise China's mandatory retirement age. Such a move is seen as a means to alleviate the growing pressure on the pension system, allowing it to remain sustainable. Additionally, it would enable pension funds to invest for longer periods, potentially yielding higher returns and contributing to the financial stability of the system. Reforming retirement age policies in China is therefore viewed as a pressing necessity to address these challenges and ensure the long-term viability of the pension system.

While the pension system is significant aspects of the challenge posed by increasing dependency to working ages, it can be influenced and managed to some extent through national-level policies and reforms. The most critical factor contributing to China's ongoing decline in its working-age population is, however, the country's economic growth.

On the one hand, new college graduates are facing growing challenges in securing employment opportunities. On the other hand, the industrial sector is grappling with a shortage of skilled labour. This divergence underscores the inherent complexities in the Chinese labour market, which is experiencing increasingly prominent structural contradictions. According to the Ministry of Human Resources and Social Security,[16] China has "over 200 million skilled workers on the Chinese mainland by far, among whom more than 50 million are highly-skilled workers". Given China's current stage of development, there remains a crucial need

---

[16] Ministry of Human Resources and Social Security. 2021. "Number of Skilled Workers in China Exceeds 200 Million." *People's Daily* (*Renmin ribao*) published on 24 March 2021. Available at http://english.www.gov.cn/news/topnews/202103/24/content_WS605a9778c6d0719374afb4dc.html, accessed 15 August 2023.

for an adequate supply of industrial workers. These workers play a key role in facilitating the country's industrial transformation and elevating it to a high-income economic economy.

## BIRTH RATE RESPONSES TO THE TWO-CHILD POLICIES

### Socio-economic Transformations and Their Impact on Birth Rate Responses

As one can tell, China experienced its most rapid economic growth and social development primarily during the 1990s through the early 2010s. Increasing income level and living standard has raised the opportunity cost higher that reduces birth in China. These profound socio-economic changes, combined with the stringent one-child policy in place, accelerated demographic transition in the country, placed China's fertility and birth rates on a continuous declining trajectory since the mid-1980s. Statistic data indicate that the population easing policies implemented after 2013 have yielded limited effects. By the end of 2022, the total number of new-borns after the conditional two-child policy was 119.3 million.[17] Seemingly, Chinese demographers' expectations of the impact of population easing policies have been overly optimistic,[18] given the observed outcomes.

However, the evaluation of the effectiveness of two-child policies has mostly focused on their nationwide outcomes, often assuming an indiscriminate impact across the entire population. This approach tends to overlook the diverse groups within the population with varying socio-economic characteristics and distinct domains of reproductive decision-making. Such research results may inadvertently neglect the nuances among different population segments, potentially leading to biases, especially towards larger populations undergoing more rapid income transitions with regional variations. Because fertility desires and the factors influencing them can vary significantly among different population groups. These differences may be further influenced by the rapidly

---

[17] From 2014 to 2021, China witnessed the birth of a total of 119.3 million new-borns under the conditional two-child policy. Following the introduction of the universal two-child policy from 2015 to 2021, the number of new-borns was to 103.3 million.

[18] Shi, Renbing, Ning Chen and Qiyu Zheng. 2018. "Zhongguo shengyu zhengce tiaozheng xiaoguo pinggu (Evaluation on the Effect of Childbearing Policy Adjustments in China)." *Zhongguo renkou kexue* (*Chinese Journal of Population Science*) 4: 114–125.

changing socio-economic conditions, including interregional labour force movements and corresponding changes in income levels.

For instance, the population displacement caused by wage gap predominantly affects young and middle-aged migrant workers, who constitute the primary reproductive demographic within society. In comparison with economically advanced regions, labour tends to migrate from low-income areas, where higher fertility desires are often retained. Thus, an increase in wage income can promptly stimulate the reproductive intentions of migrant families, thereby leading to an overall rise in birth rates within these regions experiencing labour outflows. However, this positive effect may be offset by negative consequences in other regions. As a result, the overall evaluation of the policy at the national level may be skewed, as the impact of wage gap-induced population flows can vary significantly across different geographical areas.

So, in this section, the demographic changes in China are examined within the framework of evolving socio-economic conditions and their association with population policies. Additionally, this section highlights the pertinent issue of disparities in policy effectiveness, resulting in the emergence of heterogeneous groups characterized by varying degrees of positive and/or negative responses to the two-child policies.

Empirical evidence of the current distribution of birth rates indicates that the two-child policies have imposed a positive impact on many secondary provinces situated along the East and Southeast coast of China. In these regions, where the level of per capita income remains moderate, the local residents' fertility desires have largely been preserved. The significant relaxation of the one-child policy, coupled with a reduction in the income gap due to increased migrant incomes in these regions, has led to the release of family fertility intentions. This, in turn, has generated a positive response characterized by higher birth rates in response to the implementation of the two-child policies.

It is noteworthy that in Fig. 4.6 illustrates significant fluctuations in China's birth rate during the early to mid-2010s. There were minor rebound periods following the implementation of both the conditional and universal two-child policies. After the introduction of the conditional two-child policy, the birth rate experienced a swift rebound, rising from 1.21% in 2013 to 1.24% in 2014. Similarly, following the enactment of the universal two-child policy, the birth rate increased from 1.2% in 2015 to 1.3% in 2016. However, these periods of increase were followed by a continued downward trend in the birth rate. Specifically, the birth rate decreased to 1.0% in 2019 and further declined to 0.8% in 2021.

In contrast to the prevailing notion that the two-child policies have had minimal impact on altering fertility and birth rates in contemporary China, these two instances of rebound suggest that the relaxation of the one-child policy might have fortuitously influenced certain key factors. These influences appear to have temporarily interrupted the declining trend in China's birth rate.

Taking into account that household decision-making is significantly influenced by socio-economic status and the broader macroeconomic environment, urbanization change is used as a proxy for evaluating changes in China's social and economic structures. Figure 4.6 confirms the correlation between the fertility behaviours of the Chinese population and these social structural changes.

As is shown in the figure, birth rates and urbanization trends exhibit a relatively loose connection before 2009. Intriguingly, after 2009, birth rates display a strong and consistent correlation with urbanization patterns up to recent years. This alignment can be attributed to several factors. Firstly, as China transitioned to upper-middle-income status towards

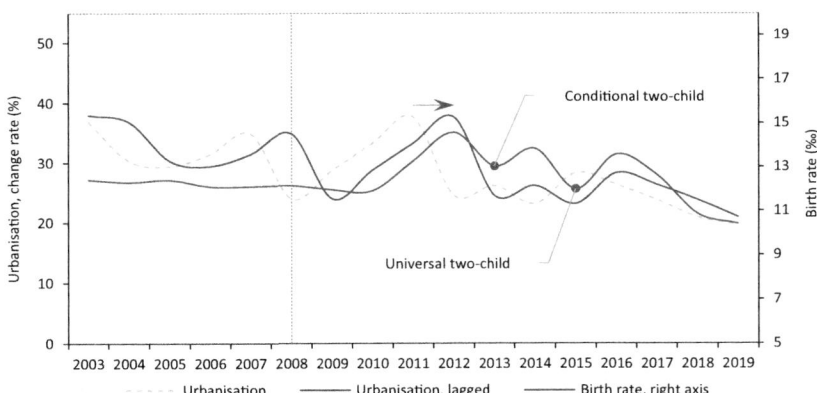

**Fig. 4.5** Birth rate and urbanization change (*Source* National Bureau of Statistics of China. (n.d.). *Zhongguo renkou he jiuye tongji nianjian* (*China Population and Employment Statistics Yearbook*). Beijing: China Statistics Press; National Bureau of Statistics of China. (n.d.). *Zhongguo tongji nianjian* (*China Statistical Yearbook*). Beijing: China Statistics Press)

the end of the 2000s, rapid improvements in living standards (e.g. increased income and savings), alongside adjustments in rural–urban structural dynamics, significantly influenced family-related behaviours and household decision-making.

The first rise of birth rates in 2012 is resulted from a combination of fast increase in per capita income right after China's elevation to the upper-middle-income category and cultural preferences, wherein most people preferred to have babies born in the year of Dragon (2012).[19] However, subsequent two rebounds in birth rates in 2014 and 2016 are likely the outcomes of a complex interplay between economic and social structural changes in response to the Chinese government's implementation of the two-child policies. These two subsequent rebounds in birth rates in 2014 and 2016 can be attributed to a combination of factors, including:

- The immediate release of fertility demands as a short-term effect: The relaxation of the one-child policy, particularly the introduction of the two-child policies, led to an immediate response from couples who had delayed or limited their family planning due to the one-child restrictions. This resulted in a short-term surge in births as families embraced the newfound opportunity to have additional children.
- And factors influencing long-term family decisions stemming from income changes and population displacement driven by interregional and rural–urban structural transformation: In the long term, economic changes, such as rising income levels, and the ongoing changes in population dynamics driven by interregional and rural–urban structural transformations have played a significant role in shaping household decision-making. As people's economic conditions improved and as they migrated to urban areas, their family planning choices evolved accordingly.

Both the short-term and long-term effects of these policies face a common challenge in contemporary China: the need for policies that are not only pertinent but also tailored to specific demographic groups and

---

[19] In Chinese societies where the culture is collective, it is believed that those born under the zodiac sign of dragon are destined to be successful and wealthy.

regions over the long term. Nonetheless, conducting a comprehensive analysis of the factors contributing to these short-term birth rate rebounds in 2014 and 2016 provides valuable insights for guiding the effectiveness of future population policies.

### *Effect of the Post-2013 Population Policies*

Excluding regions where the local population consists of more than 45% minority ethnic groups,[20] Table 4.2 assesses the impact of the two-child policies in areas that were previously subject to stringent one-child regulations. After controlling for economic development indicators, column (1) shows a significant coefficient of –2.08 for areas previously governed by the one-child rule. This suggests that the birth rate in regions previously under the one-child policy is apparently lower. When social development indicators, family properties, and household finance (column 2) are incorporated in estimation, the birth rate responses in areas formerly subject to the one-child rule worsen, with a coefficient of –2.11.

Given that regions under the one-child rule may share common customs that influence birth rates and that these customs can change over time, the impact of the two-child policies on promoting birth rates during a specific period may not be random. To address this problem, three policy dummy variables are constructed for a fixed-time analysis. These variables represent the periods as follows: two years before the 2013 conditional two-child policy, two years during 2013–2015, and two years after an area became fully open to the universal two-child rules after 2015. This allows to account for the potential non-random influence of these policies over time.

As is shown in columns (3) and (4), when household income and consumption are incorporated into estimation, there are notable changes in the signs of all three policy time dummies. These dummies, which were previously insignificant (in column 3), now exhibit significant effects (in column 4). Particularly, the coefficient for "two years after" the two-child

---

[20] The One-child policy was enforced across the majority of the Chinese population, with exceptions made for minority ethnic groups to safeguard their preservation in China. When one member of a couple belonged to a minority ethnic group, the one-child rule did not apply to this couple. Consequently, in areas where over 45% of the local population belonged to minority ethnic groups, the one-child rule did not affect more than 90% of the local population.

**Table 4.2**  Effects of the two-child policies

|  | OLS | | Fixed Time Effect | |
|---|---|---|---|---|
|  | Birth Rate | Birth Rate | Birth Rate | Birth Rate |
|  | (1) | (2) | (3) | (4) |
| Areas under One-child rule | -2.08*** | -2.11*** |  |  |
|  | (0.36) | (0.35) |  |  |
| Two Years before 2013 |  |  | -1.04 | -2.18** |
|  |  |  | (0.88) | (1.04) |
| Two Years during 2013–2015 |  |  | -0.96 | -2.52* |
|  |  |  | (1.12) | (1.33) |
| Two Years after 2015 |  |  | -0.98 | -2.80* |
|  |  |  | (1.25) | (1.47) |
| Economic Environment |  |  |  |  |
| GDP Growth | 0.03** | 0.02** | 0.02 | 0.01 |
|  | (0.01) | (0.01) | (0.02) | (0.02) |
| GDP Per Capita | 2.21*** | 1.57*** | 1.05 | 1.65 |
|  | (0.35) | (0.32) | (1.11) | (1.01) |
| Urbanization | -0.16*** | -0.07*** | 0.03 | 0.03 |
|  | (0.01) | (0.02) | (0.04) | (0.04) |
| Industrialization | -0.02 | 0.07*** | 0.05 | 0.06* |
|  | (0.03) | (0.02) | (0.04) | (0.04) |
| Social Environment |  |  |  |  |
| Primary Education |  | 0.04 |  | -0.02 |
|  |  | (0.02) |  | (0.05) |
| Tertiary Education |  | -3.62 |  | 1.16 |
|  |  | (2.40) |  | (3.23) |

(continued)

**Table 4.2** (continued)

| | OLS | | Fixed Time Effect | |
| --- | --- | --- | --- | --- |
| | Birth Rate | Birth Rate | Birth Rate | Birth Rate |
| | (1) | (2) | (3) | (4) |
| Long-Term Labour Inflow | | -0.02 | | -0.04* |
| | | (0.02) | | (0.02) |
| Short-Term Labour Inflow | | 0.67*** | | -0.03 |
| | | (0.16) | | (0.09) |
| Family Indicators | | | | |
| Male/Female Ratio | | 0.30*** | | 0.13* |
| | | (0.03) | | (0.06) |
| Dependency Ratio, Elderly | | 0.14*** | | 0.17* |
| | | (0.04) | | (0.09) |
| Total Number of Family Members | | 3.61*** | | 0.52 |
| | | (0.34) | | (0.55) |
| Year | | | Ctrl | Ctrl |
| Constant | 0.15 | -49.05*** | -4.91 | -24.76** |
| | (3.23) | (5.62) | (8.42) | (9.55) |
| Observations | 403 | 403 | 403 | 403 |
| R-squared | 0.47 | 0.72 | 0.22 | 0.28 |

*Notes* Standard errors are reported in parentheses; *** $p < 0.01$, significant at 1%; ** $p < 0.05$, significant at 5%; * $p < 0.1$, significant at 10%

policies demonstrate a significant negative impact on promoting the birth rate in regions previously subject to the one-child rule, with a coefficient of –2.80.

Furthermore, the level of regional industrialization shows a weak positive effect on the birth rate, with a one percentage point increase in industrialization associated with a 0.06 percentage point increase in the regional birth rate (column 4). Interestingly, the empirical results with policy dummies do not reveal a strong correlation between birth rate and regional economic growth (i.e. GDP growth rate and per capita GDP in column 3). Additionally, they do not support a significant educational effect on birth rate change (i.e. primary and tertiary education in column 4).

Unexpectedly, a higher elderly dependency ratio, which is supposed to negatively associated with fertility desire, has shown a significant opposite effect on the birth rate (in column 4).

## EFFECTIVENESS AND INEFFECTIVENESS OF THE TWO-CHILD POLICIES

### The Rural–Urban Divide in Birth Rate Change

The two-child policies were introduced in the context of a slowly growing labour supply and an aging population with the aim of boosting the national birth rate and preserving the fertility of the current population for future labour force growth. Fundamentally, the intention behind the two-child policies differs significantly from previous population policies, as they were expected to rapidly increase the number of new-borns.

The research discrepancy that characterizes the different functional mechanisms between birth control and birth encouraging policies likely arises from the inherent difficulties in testing theories within the framework adopted by previous research. This framework may not adequately capture the distinct working mechanisms through which the effects of different population policies are revealed. As a result, a methodological question emerges regarding whether the transmission mechanism of two-child policies differs from that of conventional population policies.

While stringent contraceptive birth control policies can immediately restrict Chinese people's fertility behaviour, the impact of encouraging population policies would primarily depend on regional development levels and the characteristics of different family groups. This implies that the effectiveness of encouraging population policies is influenced by a more complex interplay of factors compared to the straightforward impact of restrictive birth control policies.

To account for the growth and income effects on population groups with varying economic attributes, household survey data have been collected from the fifth, sixth and seventh population census.[21] These data are employed to differentiate the influences of different economic attributes on household fertility decision-making, both by gender and by sector. In this context, family system characteristics, such as household finances, are integrated into the birth rate analysis following the implementation of the two-child policies. Table 4.2 conducts the regression process, taking into consideration both sector-specific and gender-specific differences in determining an individual's fertility behaviour (Table 4.3).

The results in Table 4.2 highlight the significant impact of socioeconomic development on China's general birth rate. On average, macroeconomic growth and family characteristics exhibit positive effects on promoting the birth rate, in contrast to social development and household financial indicators. When looking at the rural–urban divide in columns (1)–(2) and (3)–(4), the significance of the rural–urban disparity becomes evident:

- The primary education enrolment rate increases urban birth rates but decreases rural birth rates.
- The elderly dependency burden significantly limits urban birth rates, while it has a weak but opposite effect on increasing birth decisions in rural families.

In addition,

---

[21] Population Census Office of the State Council, and the Department of Population and Employment of the National Bureau of Statistics of China. 2002. *Tabulation of Population Censuses of People's Republic of China 2000*. Beijing: China Statistics Press. Population Census Office of the State Council, and the Department of Population and Employment of the National Bureau of Statistics of China. 2012. *Tabulation of Population Censuses of People's Republic of China 2010*. Beijing: China Statistics Press. Population Census Office of the State Council, and the Department of Population and Employment of the National Bureau of Statistics of China. 2022. *Tabulation of Population Censuses of People's Republic of China 2020*. Beijing: China Statistics Press.

**Table 4.3** Sectoral- and sex-specific differences in birth rate changes

| | Birth rate | | | |
| | Urban | | Rural | |
| | Man (1) | Woman (2) | Man (3) | Woman (4) |
| --- | --- | --- | --- | --- |
| Economic Environment | | | | |
| GDP Growth | 0.02 (0.02) | 0.01 (0.02) | -0.01 (0.02) | 0.01 (0.02) |
| GDP Per Capita | 0.60 (0.71) | 0.60 (0.69) | 3.07*** (0.76) | 2.90*** (0.75) |
| Urbanization Rate | -0.07*** (0.02) | -0.07*** (0.02) | -0.18*** (0.02) | -0.18*** (0.02) |
| Industrialization | -0.01 (0.02) | 0.01 (0.02) | 0.06** (0.03) | 0.06** (0.03) |
| Social Environment | | | | |
| Primary Education | 0.13*** (0.03) | 0.12*** (0.03) | -0.04** (0.02) | -0.05** (0.02) |
| Tertiary Education | -0.05 (0.04) | -0.12*** (0.04) | 0.10 (0.15) | 0.16 (0.12) |
| Long-Term Labour Inflow | 0.95*** (0.34) | 1.21*** (0.37) | 2.52*** (0.38) | 2.63*** (0.38) |
| Short-Term Labour Inflow | 0.02 (0.02) | -0.02 (0.02) | 0.04 (0.03) | 0.06** (0.02) |
| Family Indicators | | | | |
| Male/Female Ratio | 0.11*** (0.02) | 0.11*** (0.02) | 0.18*** (0.03) | 0.19*** (0.03) |

(continued)

Table 4.3 (continued)

| | Birth rate | | | |
| | Urban | | Rural | |
| | Man (1) | Woman (2) | Man (3) | Woman (4) |
|---|---|---|---|---|
| Dependency Ratio, Elderly | -0.15*** | -0.10** | 0.06** | 0.07*** |
| | (0.05) | (0.05) | (0.03) | (0.03) |
| Total Number of Family Members | 0.38** | 0.34** | 0.31* | 0.30* |
| | (0.15) | (0.15) | (0.16) | (0.16) |
| Household finance | | | | |
| Per Capita Disposal Income | 0.78 | 0.49 | -1.26* | -1.20 |
| | (0.97) | (0.95) | (0.74) | (0.73) |
| Per Capita Consumption | -0.13*** | -0.14*** | -0.01 | -0.01 |
| | (0.03) | (0.03) | (0.01) | (0.01) |
| Constant | -4.00 | 1.61 | -26.20*** | -26.93*** |
| | (7.67) | (7.56) | (6.38) | (6.32) |
| Observations | 364 | 364 | 364 | 364 |
| R-squared | 0.59 | 0.60 | 0.51 | 0.52 |

*Notes* Standard errors are reported in parentheses; *** $p < 0.01$, significant at 1%; ** $p < 0.05$, significant at 5%; * $p < 0.1$, significant at 10%

- Regional GDP per capita and industrial development have significantly promoted birth rates only in rural China.
- Household consumption does not affect rural families, but it largely lowers urban families' fertility decisions.

Nevertheless, there are some indicators that work across rural and urban sectors, including:

- Long-term migration inflows have significantly increased regional birth rates.
- Family size, indicating that families with more generations tend to have more children, influences both rural and urban sectors.

Take a closer look at male–female fertility differentials. Columns (1), (3) and (2), (4) of Table 4.2 examine the fertility decision-making of men and women by incorporating gender-based family survey data[22]:

- Family indicators and household finance generally have a greater impact on either promoting or deterring men's decision-making regarding family fertility behaviours.
- Social development indicators (e.g. educational factors and labour inflows) seem to affect women more deeply than men within the family.

The results indicate that both male and female groups have responded similarly to rural–urban structural transformations, its resultant population displacement (e.g. short and/or long-term labour inflows), and income changes. Specifically:

---

[22] Office of the Leading Group of the State Council for the Seventh National Population Census. 2022. *China Population Census Yearbook 2020*. Beijing: China Statistics Press. Available at http://www.stats.gov.cn/sj/pcsj/rkpc/7rp/indexch.htm, accessed 15 August 2023. Office of the Leading Group of the State Council for the Sixth National Population Census. 2012. *China Population Census Yearbook 2010*. Beijing: China Statistics Press. Available at http://www.stats.gov.cn/sj/pcsj/rkpc/6rp/indexch.htm, accessed 15 August 2023. Office of the Leading Group of the State Council for the Fifth National Population Census. 2002. *China Population Census Yearbook 2000*. Beijing: China Statistics Press. Available at http://www.stats.gov.cn/sj/pcsj/rkpc/5rp/index.htm, accessed 15 August 2023.

- Rural populations are more sensitive to macroeconomic changes and short-term labour inflows (columns 3–4) resulting from regional urbanization.
- In contrast, both male and female groups in the urban sector responded more effectively to changes in their household financial conditions (columns 1–2).

The implementation of indiscriminate two-child policies has had a better impact on rural families, resulting in a more pronounced increase in the national birth rate. Additionally, it appears that populations residing in rapidly transitioning areas, where individuals are transitioning from rural to urban sectors, are playing a significant role as the primary drivers of the national birth rate surge.

In comparison, and in a logically expected manner, the fluctuations in birth rates within the urban population appear to be less influenced by regional urbanization. Instead, they exhibit a significant correlation with household expenditure and the intergenerational structure of families, such as the elderly dependency ratio. These findings indicate that the indiscriminate application of two-child policies has essentially equalized the impact on reproductive intentions across population groups, mitigating the disparities in their willingness to have children.

One reason that can explain this phenomenon is the implicit assumption underlying studies on the effects of the two-child policy. It was assumed that the transmission mechanism leading to an increase in birth rates following the relaxation of policies was identical, implying that population easing policies would exert the same effect on different population groups across various regions. However, in reality, this assumption does not hold true. After decades of economic growth, regional disparities in income have widened significantly, leading to variations in the attitudes of local populations towards the two-child policies. Put differently, the impact of the two-child policies may be predominantly regional in nature, with limited effects on specific population groups, rather than a nationwide, indiscriminate influence.

Empirical studies support a similar conclusion.[23] Thirty years after the implementation of the one-child policy, gender preference is no longer a significant factor in China's reproductive decision-making. Quite the contrary, "girl preference" has emerged in some regions in today's China, a departure from the preference for boys in traditional Chinese society before 1980. Consequently, gender preference and expectations have become weak factors in determining today's birth rates in China.

One of the findings indicates that regions with higher fertility levels tend to have better fertility custom, maintaining a positive regional fertility willingness that contributes to increased local birth rates following the implementation of two-child policies. Among various reasons for not having additional child, the optimal family size has emerged as a new concern for younger generation. Some studies have demonstrated that across the country, groups of young people subjectively perceive that they have reached the ideal optimal family size as a primary reason for not having additional child, rather than being restricted by economic reasons.

In practice, socio-economic changes that are indifferent across different countries have proven insufficient to reverse the prevailing downward trend in birth rates. This observation aligns with the findings discussed in Chapter 3. However, when considering the timing of policy implementation, as well as household financial circumstances and rural–urban distinctions, there emerge some positive effects on birth rate increases following the implementation of the two-child policies. This trend is in line with the small upward rebounds depicted in Fig. 4.1. In essence, the upturn in birth rates could potentially be attributed to families' decisions influenced by their altered financial conditions, which have been brought about by the rapid social and economic changes, such as regional industrialization and urbanization.

### The Regional Disparity in Birth Rate Changes Since 2013

As a result, the consequences of the two-child policies may have significant disparities across different regions. If the observed positive correlation between the two-child policies and changes in birth rates within certain

[23] For example, Li, Jieyu, and Zhang Wang. 2023. "San hai zhengce xia chengshi qingnian shengyu pianhao yu shengyu jihua (Fertility Preference and Intention of Urban Youth under the Three-Child Policy)." *Nanfang renkou* (*South China Population*) 38(3): 53–67.

groups or regions is primarily attributable to a sudden "relaxing" influence, it raises the possibility of a region- and population-specific policy effect. In this scenario, the positive effects observed in specific regions and population groups could potentially be offset or attenuated by the effects experienced by the rest of the population, ultimately rendering the national-level results statistically insignificant.

Given the imperative of relaxing population policies to effectively stimulate the birth rate for the purpose of augmenting future labour force availability and aligning with labour demand, it becomes essential to generate a sufficient number of births in regions experiencing rapid population outflows. In essence, beyond mere changes in birth rates, the manner in which increased fertility and new-borns are distributed holds significant relevance for China's population policies and the country's future economic demographics.

Figures 4.5 and 4.6 presented below, respectively illustrate the response of China's provincial birth rates to the implementation of the two-child policies and the total count of new-borns in each province, organized in descending order according to provincial GDP rankings. Additionally, within both figures, the top ten largest traditional labour-sending provinces are identified by name.[24]

In Fig. 4.7, the impact of the two-child policies becomes evident, with an overall positive effect observed in provinces such as Shandong and Guangdong. Conversely, negative responses were found in most inner and northern regions, including Hunan, Henan, and Heilongjiang. For the majority of provinces in China, the overall changes in birth rates remained limited, and in many cases, average birth rates experienced

---

[24] According to the 2000, 2010 and 2020 population censuses, the 10 provinces that experienced the highest levels of out-migration during the three decades spanning from the 1990s to the 2010s can be listed sequentially as follows: Sichuan, Anhui, Henan, Hunan, Jiangxi, Hubei, Guangxi, Guizhou, Hebei and Jiangsu. This has been calculated based on information sourced from Office of the Leading Group of the State Council for the Seventh National Population Census. 2022. *China Population Census Yearbook 2020*. Beijing: China Statistics Press. Available at http://www.stats.gov.cn/sj/pcsj/rkpc/7rp/ind exch.htm, accessed 15 August 2023. Office of the Leading Group of the State Council for the Sixth National Population Census. 2012. *China Population Census Yearbook 2010*. Beijing: China Statistics Press. Available at http://www.stats.gov.cn/sj/pcsj/rkpc/6rp/ind exch.htm, accessed 15 August 2023. Office of the Leading Group of the State Council for the Fifth National Population Census. 2002. *China Population Census Yearbook 2000*. Beijing: China Statistics Press. Available at http://www.stats.gov.cn/sj/pcsj/rkpc/5rp/index.htm, accessed 15 August 2023.

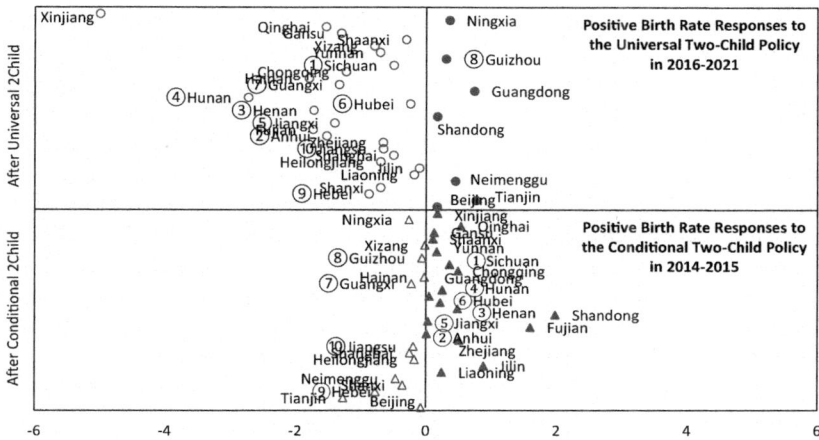

**Fig. 4.6** Responses of birth rate to the "Conditional" (2014–2015) and "Universal" Two-Child Policies (2016–2021) (*Notes* The response of birth rates to the 2013 conditional two-child policy was assessed by computing the average of changes in provincial birth rates for the years 2014 and 2015. Similarly, the birth rate responses to the 2015 universal two-child policy were determined by calculating the average estimates based on data from 2016 to 2021. *Source* National Bureau of Statistics of China. (n.d.). *Zhongguo renkou he jiuye tongji nianjian* (*China Population and Employment Statistics Yearbook*). Beijing: China Statistics Press; National Bureau of Statistics of China. (n.d.). *Zhongguo tongji nianjian* (*China Statistical Yearbook*). Beijing: China Statistics Press)

negative changes especially following the implementation of the universal two-child policy in 2015. Among the traditional labour-sending regions, only Guizhou exhibited a notable increase in birth rates. However, in all other labour-sending provinces, the two-child policies had an overall negative effect on altering local fertility preferences.

While birth rates have shown significant increases in Shandong and Guangdong, it is essential to recognize that cross-province labour mobility in these two regions remains low. Over the period of the 1990s to the 2010s, for every 100 migrant workers in China, only three originated from Shandong, and merely one came from Guangdong. This suggests that while the two-child policies may have boosted fertility desires in specific areas, their impact on labour migration to regions experiencing labour shortages may be limited when these new-borns eventually enter the labour market in the 2030s.

Traditional populous regions, particularly in the Midwest and North-east of China, displayed adverse effects in response to the two-child policies, as depicted in Fig. 4.7. These outcomes underscore that the relatively sluggish economic growth in Northeast and Midwest China has rendered the two-child policies incapable of generating a positive income effect that would stimulate higher birth rates in these regions. Conversely, Jiangsu and Zhejiang are currently undergoing a notable demographic transition, where rising per capita income is correlated with declining fertility rates. Consequently, the impact of the two-child policies on these two affluent regions has been limited. In fact, birth rates in Jiangsu and Zhejiang have been significantly influenced by the implementation of the two-child policies, but the effect has been negative in nature.

Interestingly, a noteworthy trend emerges as we observe that the majority of individuals who exhibited a positive response to the two-child policies originate from second-tier provinces situated adjacent to the eastern and southeastern coastal provinces. This phenomenon can be attributed to the rapid economic growth, local advancements, and wage improvements resulting from labour migration, all of which have acted as catalysts for increasing fertility desires among residents of these second-tier provinces subsequent to the implementation of the two-child policies. The notable rise in birth rates in these regions is evidently a direct consequence of the relaxation of regional fertility controls, serving as an extension of the emerging positive correlation between income and fertility in the immediate aftermath of the two-child policies.

Furthermore, Fig. 4.7 illustrates the relationship between the total number of new-borns born after the relaxation of the one-child policy at the provincial level and the respective local GDP levels in the year 2021, presented in descending order. This trend highlights that the population policy adjustments in China have exerted a more significant influence on the economically developed regions of the country. Children born in less economically advanced areas are more inclined to enter the industrial sector, given that the per capita income in economically advanced regions tends to surpass industrial wages.

Recall that, alongside the one-child policy, another pivotal factor that has played a substantial role in shaping post-reform demographics is the intersectoral and interregional labour migration driven by income gap. It is common to assume that increases in income have contributed to an overall decline in birth rates, especially in the case of China. However, this assumption holds true only for select regions. Even in urban China,

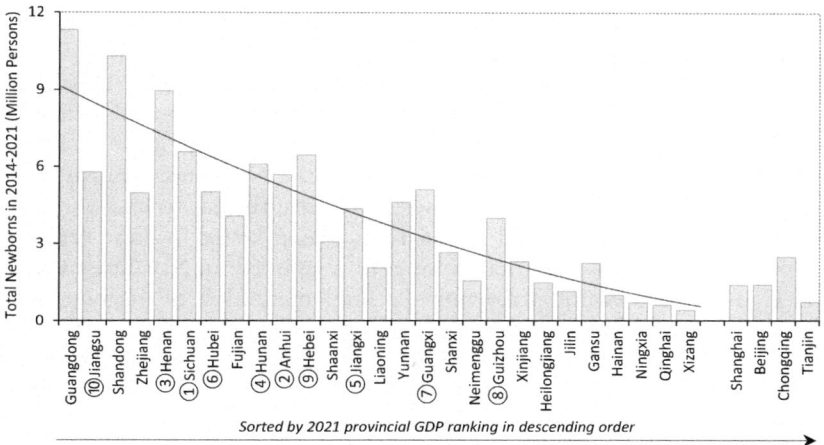

Sorted by 2021 provincial GDP ranking in descending order

**Fig. 4.7** Provincial number of new-borns after the ease of the One-Child Policy, 2014–2021 (*Notes* The total number of new-borns after 2013 was calculated by aggregating the births reported for the years 2014 through 2021, as sourced from the *China Population and Employment Statistics Yearbook* and the *China Statistical Yearbook*. It is worth noting that this calculation excludes directly controlled municipalities in China, namely Shanghai, Beijing, Tianjin, and Chongqing, which are predominantly oriented towards the service sector. *Source* National Bureau of Statistics of China. (n.d.). *Zhongguo renkou he jiuye tongji nianjian* (*China Population and Employment Statistics Yearbook*). Beijing: China Statistics Press; National Bureau of Statistics of China. (n.d.). *Zhongguo tongji nianjian* (*China Statistical Yearbook*). Beijing: China Statistics Press; Office of the Leading Group of the State Council for the Seventh National Population Census. 2022. *China Population Census Yearbook 2020*. Beijing: China Statistics Press. Available at http://www.stats.gov.cn/sj/pcsj/rkpc/7rp/indexch.htm, accessed 15 August 2023)

including the affluent eastern coastal areas where living standards have reached upper-middle-income levels and beyond, this trend is primarily evident in the richest provinces, such as Jiangsu and Zhejiang. Consequently, the modern demographic transition theory alone cannot fully account for the variations in birth rate responses to the two-child policies across different regions in China.

However, the outcomes deviated from the expectations of policymakers. The responses in both economically advanced regions, such as

Jiangsu and Zhejiang, and the least developed regions, including the Northeast and Midwest China, were negative to the two-child policies. This resulted in fewer new-borns in populous regions like Northeast China and Gansu, as well as economically advanced regions like Jiangsu and Zhejiang when compared to provinces like Guangdong and Shandong. The slower growth of income levels in the Northeast and Midwest China meant that the two-child policies were insufficient to create a positive income effect that would stimulate increased births in these regions. This also explains why the total number of new-borns in Northeast China and Gansu remained low following the implementation of the two-child policies. Conversely, Jiangsu and Zhejiang are undergoing a significant demographic transition, wherein rising per capita income is associated with declining fertility rates. Consequently, the two-child policies have had limited impact in these two affluent regions.

Given the reality that the majority of labour-sending regions remain less developed, the declining birth rates would exacerbate the working-age ratio deficit in these regions, ultimately reducing the labour supply available for their development efforts in catching up with the more advanced regions. Consequently, this dynamic could lead to an expansion of the regional income gap in China. However, under current circumstances, less developed labour-sending provinces, such as Guangxi, Jiangxi, and Anhui, continue to play a significant role in shaping China's labour market structure. This is due to the fact that the costs associated with promoting fertility in these areas are lower, primarily stemming from relatively lower living expenses and thus, lower income expectations.

Indeed, it is conventionally understood that income increases have played a significant role in contributing to the prevailing low fertility rates in China. This understanding is particularly applicable to urban China, especially the affluent eastern coastal regions where living standards have attained upper-middle-income levels and beyond. However, it is important to acknowledge that income distribution in China remains skewed, with a large portion of the population—approximately **600 million individuals**—earning a monthly income lower than **CN¥1000 yuan** (approximately US$140 dollars).[25] Thus relative poverty persists

[25] Li, Keqiang. 2020. "China Has Over 600 Million Poor with $140 Monthly Income: Premier Li Keqiang." Available at https://www.cnbctv18.com/economy/china-has-over-600-million-poor-with-140-monthly-income-premier-li-keqiang-6024341.htm, accessed on 15 August 2022.

in many low-income provinces, and this economic constraint hinders the increase in birth rates across most regions of China, even with the implementation of two-child policies.

In light of the responses to population easing, it is evident that while the two-child policies have had limited impact on promoting an increase in the nationwide birth rate, they have yielded distinct regional effects. Despite four decades of economic growth, the higher-income regions have been unable to generate sufficient wage pressure to attract labour into productive sectors, notably the industrial sector. This persistent labour shortage in China poses a growing challenge to the country's ongoing industrial transition, particularly as the fertility gap between low- and high-income regions continues to widen under the influence of the two-child policies.

Presently, the two and three-child policies are equally applied across the entire country, without accounting for the regional differences. In the less developed regions of the country, the relaxation of the one-child policy appears to be insufficient in addressing the fertility challenges they face. Income limitations exert a substantial influence on fertility decisions in these areas, unless the Chinese government undertakes measures to provide financial support or subsidies to alleviate the cost burden associated with childbearing in these regions.

In the context of high interregional inequality in China, any further relaxation of birth control measures could exacerbate the existing biases in the country's birth distribution. When compare the current distribution of new-borns with the regional labour distribution from four decades ago, during which a substantial number of working-age individuals migrated from underdeveloped regions in pursuit of better labour prospects, it is clear that the current patterns of new-born distribution raise concerns about the future dynamics of China's labour market.

As evident, most regions that traditionally send labour have already grappled with the challenges posed by local aging populations. China's current working-age population has reached a turning point, signifying a fundamental shift in its labour market dynamics towards a situation of persistent labour shortage. While the government is compelled to implement measures to stimulate childbirth, it is imperative to recognize that population encouragement policies must incorporate a more robust incentive plan and a targeted policy design to effectively address the disparities in the childbearing-aged population. In the context of declining labour supply, adjustments within and between different segments of the labour market become particularly important for China to successfully complete its industrial upgrade and ascend to the high-income group category.

## SUMMARY

This chapter delves into China's demographic transition in the context of the state's evolving population policies closely intertwined with economic imperatives. As the Chinese population encounters rapidly evolving socio-economic conditions and shifts in population policies, variations in family structures and household finances play a pivotal role in shaping individuals' decisions on reproduction. Through an in-depth analysis of inter-regional differences among provinces, this chapter reveals that China's regional birth desires and fertility rates are characterized by significant differentiations. The income gap, as well as income-induced labour migration and population redistribution, collectively contribute to the diverse responses in birth rates observed following the population easing policies implemented after 2013.

In contrast to regional variations, the national birth rate has displayed a consistent declining trend, presenting a challenge to China's ongoing economic transition as it grapples with an impending labour shortage. The Chinese economy, marked by its remarkable growth momentum since the reform era, is now transitioning into a growth pattern constrained by labour availability. Interestingly, despite the interregional disparities, they have not translated into a general increase in birth rates nationwide. The rapid urbanization process, which improved the affordability of additional children for rural populations, has concurrently reshaped the country's fertility landscape, leading to heightened fertility desires in certain regions and population segments.

Developed countries often address labour shortages by engaging in industrial transfers and leveraging resultant technology upgrades. However, China faces a different challenge—a scarcity of essential labour inputs required to sustain its ongoing transition. In a scenario of declining total labour supply, the ability to manage and make adjustments within and between various segments of the labour market becomes particularly important. Therefore, for China, the key question concerning its current labour market pertains to whether the newly added labour force resulting from the two-child policies can effectively integrate into China's industrial workforce. This integration will be instrumental in propelling the country's continued economic and income transition.

# References

Becker, Gary S. 1981. *A Treatise on The Family*. Chicago: Harvard University Press; Becker, Gary S. 1964. *Human Capital: A Theoretical and Empirical Analysis, with Special Reference to Education*. New York: Columbia University Press; Becker, Gary S. 1976. *The Economic Approach to Human Behaviour*. Chicago: University of Chicago Press; Schultz, Theodore W. 1963. *Economic Value of Education*. New York: Columbia University Press.

Cai, Fang, and Kam Wing Chan. 2009. "The Global Economic Crisis and Unemployment in China." *Eurasian Geography and Economics* 50(5):513–531.

Cai, Fang, and Meiyan Wang. 2005. "Challenge facing China's Economic Growth in Its Aging but not Affluent Era." *China and World Economy* 14: 20–31.

Chinese Communist Party Central Committee, Document No. 15. 2013. "Zhonggong zhongyang guowuyuan yinfa guanyu tiaozheng wanshan shengyu zhengce de yijian (Opinions Issued by the CCP Central Committee and the State Council on 'Adjusting and Improving the Family Planning Policy')." Beijing: 30 December 2013.

Chinese Communist Party Central Committee, Document No. 40. 2015. "Zhonggong zhongyang guowuyuan guanyu shishi quanmian lianghai zhengce gaige wanshan jihua shengyu fuwu guanli de jueding (Decision of the Central Committee of the CCP and the State Council on Implementing the Universal Two-Child Policy and Reforming and Improving the Management of Family Planning Services)." Beijing: Chinese Communist Party Central Committee, 31 December 2015.

Du, Jane. 2017. "China's Population Policy and the Future of Its Labour Market." In Tong, Sarah Y., and Jing Wan. (eds.). *China's Economy in Transformation under the New Normal*. Singapore: World Scientific.

Li, Jieyu, and Zhang Wang. 2023. "San hai zhengce xia chengshi qingnian shengyu pianhao yu shengyu jihua (Fertility Preference and Intention of Urban Youth under the Three-Child Policy)." *Nanfang renkou (South China Population)* 38(3): 53–67.

Miller, Amalia R. 2011. "The Effects of Motherhood Timing on Career Path." *Journal of Population Economics* 24(3):1071–1100.

Ministry of Human Resources and Social Security. 2021. "Number of Skilled Workers in China Exceeds 200 Million." *People's Daily (Renmin ribao)* published on 24 March 2021. Available at http://english.www.gov.cn/news/topnews/202103/24/content_WS605a9778c6d0719374afb4dc.html, accessed 15 August 2023.

National Bureau of Statistics of China. (n.d.). *Zhongguo renkou he jiuye tongji nianjian (China Population and Employment Statistics Yearbook)*. Beijing: China Statistics Press.

National Bureau of Statistics of China. (n.d.). *Zhongguo tongji nianjian (China Statistical Yearbook)*. Beijing: China Statistics Press.

National Bureau of Statistics of China. 2019. *Migrant Workers Monitoring Survey Report 2018*. Available at http://www.stats.gov.cn/sj/zxfb/202302/t20230 203_1900299.html, accessed 15 August 2023.

National Bureau of Statistics of China. 2020. *Migrant Workers Monitoring Survey Report 2019*. Available at http://www.stats.gov.cn/sj/zxfb/202302/t20230 203_1900710.html, accessed 15 August 2023.

Office of the Leading Group of the State Council for the Fifth National Population Census. 2002. *China Population Census Yearbook 2000*. Beijing: China Statistics Press. Available at http://www.stats.gov.cn/sj/pcsj/rkpc/ 5rp/index.htm, accessed 15 August 2023.

Office of the Leading Group of the State Council for the Seventh National Population Census. 2022. *China Population Census Yearbook 2020*. Beijing: China Statistics Press. Available at http://www.stats.gov.cn/sj/pcsj/rkpc/7rp/ind exch.htm, accessed 15 August 2023.

Office of the Leading Group of the State Council for the Sixth National Population Census. 2012. *China Population Census Yearbook 2010*. Beijing: China Statistics Press. Available at http://www.stats.gov.cn/sj/pcsj/rkpc/6rp/ind exch.htm, accessed 15 August 2023.

Population Census Office of the State Council, and the Department of Population and Employment of the National Bureau of Statistics of China. 2002. *Tabulation of Population Censuses of People's Republic of China 2000*. Beijing: China Statistics Press.

Population Census Office of the State Council, and the Department of Population and Employment of the National Bureau of Statistics of China. 2012. *Tabulation of Population Censuses of People's Republic of China 2010*. Beijing: China Statistics Press.

Population Census Office of the State Council, and the Department of Population and Employment of the National Bureau of Statistics of China. 2022. *Tabulation of Population Censuses of People's Republic of China 2020*. Beijing: China Statistics Press.

Shi, Renbing, Ning Chen, and Qiyu Zheng. 2018. "Zhongguo shengyu zhengce tiaozheng xiaoguo pinggu (Evaluation on the Effect of Childbearing Policy Adjustments in China)." *Zhongguo renkou kexue (Chinese Journal of Population Science)* 4: 114–125.

The State Council Gazette No. 16. 2020. *Likeqiang zongli chuxi jizhe hui bing huida zhongwai jizhe tiwen (Premier Li Keqiang Attended the Press Conference and Answered Questions from Domestic and Foreign Reporters)*. Beijing: The State Council of People's Republic of China, 28 May 2020. Available at https://www.gov.cn/gongbao/content/2020/content_5 517496.htm, accessed on 15 August 2023.

The World Bank. (n.d.). World Development Indicators. Washington: The World Bank. Available at https://datacatalog.worldbank.org/dataset/world-develo pment-indicators, accessed 15 August 2023.

Wang, Dewen, Fang Cai, and Wenshu Gao. 2006. "Globalization and the Shortage of Rural Workers: A Macroeconomic Perspective." In Ingrid Nielsen, Russell Smyth and Marika Vicziany. (eds.). *Globalization and Labour Mobility in China*. Clayton: MAI Press.

Zeng, Yi, and Zhenglian Wang. 2014. "A Policy Analysis on Challenges and Opportunities of Population/Household Aging in China." *Journal of Population Aging* 7: 255–281.

Zhang, Xiaobo, Jin Yang, and Shenglin Wang. 2011. "China has Reached the Lewis Turning Point." *China Economic Review* 22(4):542–554; Wang, Meiyan. 2010. "The Rise of Labor Cost and the Fall of Labor Input: Has China reached Lewis Turning point?" *China Economic Journal* 3(2):137–153.

CHAPTER 5

# Conclusion

**Abstract** This chapter provides a retrospective summary of the principal themes and issues explored throughout this work.

**Keywords** Demographic trends · Economic slowdown · Labour shortage · Policy time window

## DEMOGRAPHIC TRENDS IN CHINA

Those days when "one of every three to four human being has been Chinese"[1] were seemingly a thing of the past. It has become a natural law in modern society that fertility rate would inevitably decline as industrialization progresses. In the case of China, this phenomenon has been expedited by the government's population control policies implemented, shaping a rapid reduction in China's share in the global population and a significantly compressed demographic transition compared to the rest of the world.

---

[1] Lee, James Z., and Feng Wang. 1999. *One Quarter of Humanity: Malthusian Mythology and Chinese Realities, 1700–2000.* Cambridge, MA and London.: Harvard University Press.

© The Author(s), under exclusive license to Springer Nature      149
Switzerland AG 2024
J. Du, *China's Labour Market, 1950–2050*, Palgrave Studies in
Economic History, https://doi.org/10.1007/978-3-031-53138-5_5

Population control in China traces its roots back to the ideology of CCP centred around centralized planning. The decision-makers recognized necessity of robust policies to shape the future layout of the country's demography, irrespective of the means employed. These population policies have integrated into the ruling party's quest for ideological legitimacy, founded on a classical view of socio-economic development. This view is rooted in the belief that population, in addition to capital, is consistently regarded as a pivotal component contributing to a nation's economic growth.

For China, a country that once boasted the world's largest population, labour shortages were seldom a concern. In fact, in response to the population boom experienced during the 1950s and 1960s, the Chinese government initiated a series of efforts beginning in 1962 to manage and stabilize its population size to maintain a steady state in terms of per capita resources. The culmination of these measures was the introduction of the stringent "one-child policy" in 1981. However, since the early 2010s, there have been growing calls for the Chinese government to ease population control policies, driven by the looming threat of labour shortages in China.

First, TFR has undergone a significant decline, plummeting from 6.2 in 1962 to 1.7 in the 2010s, a trend attributed to both population control measures and economic development. Second, the elderly dependent ratio has concurrently risen from 8.0 to 13.1 during the same period. Consequently, the Chinese government signalled its willingness to relax population control policies. In 2013, China initiated the first relaxation of its controversial one-child policy by permitting couples to have two children if one of the parents was an only child. Subsequently, in 2015, the central government removed this condition, extending the option of having two children to all couples. Most recently, in 2021, a three-child policy was implemented, allowing all Chinese families to have up to three children. However, it appears that the relaxation of the one-child policy has had limited impact in stimulating China's nationwide fertility and birth rates. The general fertility rate continues to decline, with only two brief upticks in response to the post-2013 population easing. Evidently, other factors are influencing a couple's decision regarding fertility.

Despite the recent relaxation of the one-child policy, the United Nation's World Population Prospects 2022[2] projects a significant reduction in China's effective labour supply, with a projected decrease of one fifth by 2050. This implies that roughly a quarter billion Chinese workers will exit the labour market by that time. An analysis of China's labour market and demographic trends suggests that the current policy adjustments are unlikely to reverse the country's declining labour supply in the near future. To counteract the looming labour shortage, more robust efforts are needed to stimulate population growth. This necessitates the liberalization of population control policies and proactive measures aimed at addressing the impending labour deficit.

In addition to policy efforts, the timing of implementation is a critical factor to consider. Over the past five decades, the population of women of childbearing age has declined significantly, with an average decrease of 21.5% every 10 years during the 1990s and 2000s. When compared to the size of the post-70s female population, the post-90s cohort has diminished by one fifth, and the post-00s generation has decreased by nearly half. Given this rapid decline in the population base of women of childbearing age, the cost of promoting population growth is poised to continuously rise. In the next decade, the post-80s and post-90s generations will move out of their childbearing years and be succeeded by the post-00s cohort in terms of population reproduction. If policies aimed at enhancing population growth are implemented after this transition, the smaller female population base may struggle to worsen the imminent sharp decline in labour supply. Therefore, it is imperative for the Chinese government to act promptly and leverage the demographic window provided by the post-80s and post-90s population cohorts, as hesitance in doing so could significantly limit the effectiveness of population enhancement policies.

---

[2] United Nations, Department of Economic and Social Affairs, Population Division. 2022. World Population Prospects 2022. Available at https://population.un.org/wpp/, accessed 15 August 2022.

# ECONOMIC DECELERATION
## AND THE IMPENDING LABOUR SHORTAGE

Demographic changes constitute a chronic concern, and population policies are inherently long-term endeavours, taking substantial time to yield significant effects and contribute to socio-economic development. The children born half a century ago in the 1970s have a direct influence on China's economic status today. Consequently, substantial and prolonged interventions in population reproduction are bound to generate enduring repercussions throughout the economic system, impacting both micro-level factors, such as household behaviours, and macro-level aspects, including the labour market and capital market. The enduring impact of these population changes may not be immediately apparent in the short term but has the potential to deliver an inevitable blow to the nation's well-being and stability over time.

China's ongoing labour shortage stemming from its one-child policy serves as a characteristic example of the consequences of population control measures. A reduction in the overall labour supply can trigger a resource outflow and result in a growth pattern constrained by labour availability, as observed in China (Bai and Zhang 2014).[3] An illustrative instance of this phenomenon can be seen in the slowdown of China's secondary industry. The dwindling working-age population and the swiftly escalating burden of old-age dependency would rapidly erode the country's advantages in labour-intensive sectors. This, in turn, may lead to reduced capital inflows, which are vital for sustaining rapid industrialization in certain cases.

China's secondary industry has already witnessed deceleration, particularly in export-led sectors that traditionally depended on abundant and low-cost labour supply. The diminishing working-age population and the swiftly increasing dependent ratio have eroded China's competitive advantages in exporting labour-intensive products. As a result, in certain cases, there has been a decline in capital inflows from foreign investors. Deeper industrialization remains pivotal to China's future growth. Access to capital inflows and technology transfers from economically advanced economies can play a crucial role in enhancing productivity, efficiency

---

[3] Bai, Chong'en and Qiong Zhang. 2014. "Zhongguo de ziben huibao lv jiqi yingxiang yinsu fenxi (Rate of Return to Capital in China and the Influencing Factors)". *Shijie jingji* (*The Journal of World Economy*) 137(10):3–30.

gains, and opportunities for innovation. These developments are vital for strengthening China's competitiveness in international markets and sustaining its growth trajectory.

The ongoing demographic changes in China may indeed open up employment opportunities in sectors like the elderly care industry. However, it also implies that there could be a shortage of labour supply in the secondary industry. While foreign labour could help fill certain gaps, especially in skilled areas, it is unlikely that the Chinese government would heavily rely on foreign labour sources, as doing so could significantly alter the country's demographic landscape. This policy stance contrasts with immigration policies in some smaller economies that actively seek and rely on foreign labour to supplement their domestic workforce.

These insights shed light on the original intentions behind the formulation and implementation of population policies, while also underscoring the profound influence of these policies on the evolution of policymakers' ideologies and decision-making processes regarding China's economic challenges at various stages of its industrialization journey. Indeed, the one-child policy effectively relieved young labour from childbearing and dependency during the 1980s to the 2000s, ensuring a continuous influx of labour that played a pivotal role in China's rapid industrialization and economic take-off. However, as China grapples with ongoing demographic shifts, it will increasingly encounter challenges in supplying the necessary labour force to sustain its economic development and income transition. These shifting demographics have far-reaching implications for the country's future economic prospects.

## INCOME TRANSITIONS AND INSIGHTS FROM ASIAN EXPERIENCES

After WWII, the concepts of income transition and income classification gained popularity as a means to assess and compare economic performance among different economies. Despite demographic shifts, evidence indicates that over the past five decades, economies in East and Southeast Asia have experienced rapid growth and have transitioned between income groups relatively swiftly. While it is true that successfully navigating the income bottleneck ultimately hinges on sustaining growth and continually enhancing living standards over time, the crucial question lies in understanding the dynamics of this process.

Economies encounter distinct challenges during various stages of their growth trajectories, offering valuable lessons for others to learn from. The income transitions observed in East and Southeast Asian economies over the years demonstrate that more economically open nations tend to undergo a faster income transition process, ultimately achieving higher living standards in post-war Asia. For non-resource-based Asian economies aiming to sustain stable and rapid growth, the adoption of new technologies becomes a key strategy to ensure their transition keeps pace with global economic advancements. Analysing the income transition experiences of East and Southeast Asian economies from 1960 to 2020 reveals that interruptions in this process were predominantly caused by factors such as domestic social movements driven by nationalism, government controls on capital inflows, inadequate responses to external economic instability (such as crises), and a failure to foster local technology upgrading. These experiences underscore the importance of addressing these challenges to ensure a smoother income transition.

Therefore, in addition to demographic considerations, the lessons learned emphasize a positive association between successful income transitions and economic openness. Economic openness plays a pivotal role by directly influencing growth and transition, facilitating the adoption of new techniques and technology-based machinery imports for rapid industrialization. For today's Asian developing economies, a significant challenge lies in establishing institutions that enable their domestic industries to keep pace with global advancements. Policy efforts targeted at the factors previously identified as contributing to growth can be particularly beneficial for Asian developing economies, including China. These policies will help them avoid stagnation at their current income levels, whether they are classified as low income, lower-middle-income, or upper-middle income. In comparison with its neighbouring countries, China has managed to remain in the upper-middle-income group even as its working-age ratio begins to decline.

This work delves into the complex interplay between demographic and economic factors in China's dual transition. It underscores how China's economic growth over the past four decades, particularly its export-led growth model, has greatly benefited from its demographic characteristics and, consequently, its labour structure. However, as the one-child generation enters the labour market, China's swiftly declining working-age ratio is reshaping the country's relative factor advantages. The shortage of sufficient labour supply since the 2010s appears to be an intercepting process that could potentially impede China's economic momentum.

Additionally, the rapid expansion of higher education has led to the accumulation of human capital in China. However, a downside to this trend is that as the share of labour with tertiary education increases, the issue of shortages in industrial workers may worsen. Unlike other inputs, the size and structure of a population are challenging to alter in the short term, rendering this problem difficult for the Chinese government to resolve. In the face of a shrinking population size and a rapidly aging demographic structure, China's ongoing income transition may become increasingly challenging to navigate.

## THE TIME WINDOW OF POPULATION POLICIES

Unlike economic policies, population policies have their unique constraints. The impact of population policies on changing fertility patterns takes years to become evident and stable, and reversing their effects can be challenging. Many of the prominent demographic characteristics in China today are a result of past population policies. For example, Mao's promotion of childbirth was considered suitable for China's post-war socio-economic conditions. However, when the baby boomers of the 1950s and 1960s started entering the workforce, the sudden increase in labour supply became a contributing factor to serious social and economic issues, including unemployment, in the 1980s and 1990s. This presented a significant challenge that could undermine the legitimacy of the Deng government and hinder the country's development. Consequently, Deng implemented the stringent one-child policy. Unlike some other policies, the effects of population policies take a generation to become noticeable in the labour market. While population policies can successfully achieve the country's initial policy goals, such as reducing the population, they cannot guarantee that these goals will still be relevant or desirable after a generation has passed. This highlights the long-term and irreversible nature of demographic changes influenced by population policies.

The Deng government believed that achieving a higher per capita resource allocation was pivotal to economic success, and they perceived a large Chinese population as an impediment to achieving this goal. The one-child policy successfully reduced birth rates, aligning with Deng's objectives. However, it also left the Xi Jinping government grappling with the consequences of a rapidly aging society and a labour market that had deteriorated significantly, a situation that may persist until at least 2050. This turbulence, driven by policy shocks and demographic changes, serves as the backdrop for China's current two-child policies and the impending need for labour market adjustments. As a decline in labour supply becomes inevitable, it becomes crucial to carefully study how to effectively adapt labour market segmentation to make efficient use of the available labour pool. This presents a complex challenge that requires thoughtful consideration and strategic planning.

Based on the estimated results of population easing policies, this work also suggests that the current two-child and three-child policies are unlikely to reverse the ongoing declines in China's birth rate, TFR, and even the overall population size. In other words, after decades of fertility control measures, having one child has become deeply ingrained as a social norm, and it would be challenging for population policies alone to change this norm in today's China. This fundamental social institution and framework have exerted a decisive influence on the country's economic transition. China's current labour market is grappling with serious structural unemployment, primarily due to the mismatch between labour supply and demand. This situation may further exacerbate the country's existing labour supply issues, leading to inefficient utilization of the available labour force. Addressing these challenges will require comprehensive strategies that extend beyond population policies.

In conclusion, if China had pursued a more gradual path of demographic change without stringent fertility control, the country's economic growth over the past four decades would likely have been much slower. On the other hand, the implementation of fertility control policies has led to the rapid aging of the population and a significantly deteriorated labour market, with a sharp decline in labour supply expected in the near future. This underscores the two-sided effects of China's stringent population policies and highlights the irreversible and determinative impact of demographics on China's dual transition.

## REFERENCES

Bai, Chong'en and Qiong Zhang. 2014. "Zhongguo de ziben huibao lv jiqi yingxiang yinsu fenxi (Rate of Return to Capital in China and the Influencing Factors)." *Shijie jingji* (*The Journal of World Economy*) 137(10):3–30.

Lee, James Z., and Feng Wang. 1999. *One Quarter of Humanity: Malthusian Mythology and Chinese Realities, 1700–2000.* Cambridge, MA and London.: Harvard University Press.

United Nations, Department of Economic and Social Affairs, Population Division. 2022. World Population Prospects 2022. Available at https://population.un.org/wpp/, accessed 15 August 2022.

# Index

Printed by Printforce, United Kingdom